PRACTICAL ILLUSTRATIONS

1 Thessalonians – Philemon

Indexed and Keyed to *The Preacher's Outline and Sermon Bible*®

Practical Illustrations

1 Thessalonians
2 Thessalonians
1 Timothy
2 Timothy
Titus
Philemon

Leadership Ministries Worldwide
Chattanooga, TN

Practical Illustrations has been compiled for God's people to use both in their personal lives and in their teaching. Leadership Ministries Worldwide wants God's people to use *Practical Illustrations*. The purpose of the copyright is to prevent the reproduction, misuse, and abuse of the material.

May our Lord bless us all as we live, preach, teach, and write for Him, fulfilling His great commission to live righteous and godly lives and to make disciples of all nations.

Please address all requests for information or permission to:
Leadership Ministries Worldwide
PO Box 21310
Chattanooga, TN 37424-0310
Ph.# (423) 855-2181   FAX (423) 855-8616   E-Mail info@outlinebible.org
http://www.outlinebible.org

Library of Congress Catalog Card Number: 2001 135014
International Standard Book Number: 978-1-57407-186-3

PRINTED IN THE U.S.A.

PUBLISHED BY LEADERSHIP MINISTRIES WORLDWIDE

3   4   5   6   7   13   14   15   16

DEDICATED

To all the men and women of the world who preach and teach the Gospel of our Lord Jesus Christ and to the Mercy and Grace of God

- Demonstrated to us in Christ Jesus our Lord.

    "In whom we have redemption through His blood, the forgiveness of sins, according to the riches of His grace." (Eph. 1:7)

- Out of the mercy and grace of God His Word has flowed. Let every person know that God will have mercy upon him, forgiving and using him to fulfill His glorious plan of salvation.

    "For God so loved the world, that he gave His only begotten Son, that whosoever believeth in Him should not perish, but have everlasting life. For God sent not his son into the world to condemn the world, but that the world through him might be saved." (Jn. 3:16-17)

    "For this is good and acceptable in the sight of God our Saviour; who will have all men to be saved, and to come unto the knowledge of the truth." (1 Tim. 2:3-4)

10/11

Practical Illustrations

has been compiled for God's servants to use in their study, teaching, and preaching of God's Holy Word...

- To share the Word of God with the world.
- To help the believer, both minister and layman alike, in his understanding, preaching, and teaching of God's Word.
- To do everything we possibly can to lead men, women, boys and girls to give their hearts and lives to Jesus Christ and to secure the eternal life which He offers.
- To do all we can to minister to the needy of the world.
- To give Jesus Christ His proper place, the place the Word gives Him. Therefore, no work of Leadership Ministries Worldwide will ever be personalized.

ABOUT
PRACTICAL ILLUSTRATIONS

This volume of *Practical Illustrations* covers 1 and 2 Thessalonians, 1 and 2 Timothy, Titus, and Philemon. You can use it alone or as a companion to other *Outline Bible* Resource Materials. This book is cross-indexed several ways to make it easy to find the illustrations you need. The following information is provided to help you use the book more effectively:

Use this index if you want to find illustrations for a particular passage of Scripture.

Each illustration or introduction includes the following elements to aid in your study and in locating the appropriate illustration, whether by topic or Scripture reference:

Key Number: Each illustration is numbered. The first digit indicates the *Practical Illustrations* volume number (which is the same as the corresponding volume of *The Preacher's Outline and Sermon Bible®*). The second digit indicates the order in which the illustration appears in *Practical Illustrations*.

Subject Heading: Each illustration is categorized by topic.

Scripture Reference: Each illustration is keyed to the Scripture passage it illustrates.

POSB Reference: This indicates where additional information can be found in *The Preacher's Outline and Sermon Bible®*.

Illustration Title: Each illustration is given an appropriate title.

Use this index if you want to find illustrations on a particular topic.

SCRIPTURE INDEX

1 THESSALONIANS

2 THESSALONIANS
ILLUSTRATIONS

1 TIMOTHY

1 TIMOTHY

2 TIMOTHY

PRACTICAL
ILLUSTRATIONS

PRACTICAL
ILLUSTRATIONS

10-100

ACCOUNTABILITY

Titus 2:1-10

A Plan to Stay Faithful

(POSB: Note 5, point 3)

Who helps you control your thought life? Whether you are old or young, man or woman, you are at the mercy of thoughts planted by the devil. But the *thought* alone—the temptation—is not where the sin lies. The sin enters when that thought is entertained and kept in the secret closet of your heart.

Two young Christian men who loved the Lord and their families saw a need for accountability to someone. They agreed to meet once a week to ask each other some hard questions. These five questions kept them on their best behavior:
1. Describe your relationship to God this past week.
2. What did you wrestle with in your thought life?
3. Are you in the center of God's will?
4. Are your relationships growing?
5. Have you been fully truthful in answering the first four questions?

Was their accountability to each other a waste of time? Was it really an act of weakness? Looking at it from a Scriptural standpoint, they proved to be smart and courageous men who knew their weaknesses. It takes a brave soul to look another person in the eye and not only *ask* the hard questions but *answer* them as well. To whom are you accountable?

ᕕ ᕗ

10-101

ANTICHRIST

2 Thessalonians 2:10-12

The Deceit of the Enemy

(POSB: Introduction)

What kind of person would ever choose to follow the antichrist? Think about it for a moment. To be a part of his group...
- would make you an enemy of God
- would mean casting away all truth for a life of deceit
- would mean choosing a life of total destruction
- would mean going down with the leader

Years ago, thousands of people followed Adolph Hitler down a blind path. This German Nazi leader gathered a committed group of disciples who never blinked an eye as millions of Jews were exterminated. After the war's conclusion, many of Hitler's followers were convicted of war crimes. They either were imprisoned or executed for their participation in Hitler's agenda.

Men like Hitler have come and gone in history. But there will come a day when one who is even more evil will come and deceive millions. They will follow him blindly—to their own destruction.

✎

10-102

ANTICHRIST

2 Thessalonians 2:4-9

(POSB: Introduction)

The Trojan Horse

Are you familiar with the term Trojan horse? You might remember from history that the Trojans were attacking, but could not conquer, the city of Sparta. Finally, the Trojans decided to trick their foes by building a hollow wooden horse large enough to hold many soldiers. This Trojan horse was presented as a peace offering. It looked innocent and peaceful on the outside. The pride of the men of Sparta got the best of them. They accepted the horse into the city gates. After nightfall, the soldiers came out of the horse and captured the city.

In the same sense, the antichrist will come into this world as a Trojan horse. People will trust him to bring peace, but he will deceive the nations of the world. How will he do this? By appearing to be the Messiah, the Savior of the world. The antichrist will actually claim to be God. Remember this: the Apostle John tells us that the spirit of the antichrist is already here (1 Jn. 4:3). We must guard against any who do not acknowledge that Jesus of Nazareth is the Christ, the only Prince of Peace, the only Savior of the world.

✎

10-103

APOSTASY

2 Thessalonians 2:1-3

(POSB: Note 2, point 1)

The Terror of Judgment

What would it be like to see millions turn away from their confession of Christ as Lord and Savior? It would be a vivid nightmare for any one of us to dream. Peek into one man's sleeping quarters. Right away you see him tossing and turning, fighting to wake up from the horror that has gripped him. Allow him to share with you his horrible dream.

It was as if the world had turned upside down. I could hardly believe my eyes as people I knew turned their backs on God. These people went to church and knew the right things to say. But all of them met together and declared to God that they intended to finish the rebellion that Lucifer and his henchmen had begun ages ago. Only this time they intended to dethrone God and to assume control of creation.

PRACTICAL ILLUSTRATIONS

Somehow I got caught up in the excitement of the meeting and began to voice my support with the others. After I yelled "Down with God!" I got a sick feeling in the pit of my stomach. My mind began to re-run old memories of all God had done for me as a child. He had healed me from a serious illness. He constantly provided food and shelter for my family and me. We never went without the necessities.

What went wrong? To tell you the truth, I went wrong. I simply got tired of living by the rules. I found it easier to follow rebels than to follow the Good Shepherd. But some things have got to change now. In my dream, the last scene made an impression on me that I will never forget.

God swept His hand into that crowd of rebels and set us up like dominos on their ends. And then, with a flick of His finger each one toppled the other. As each one fell, the earth would open up with consuming flames. I was the last domino. My eyes got bigger and bigger as the one before me tipped me over—and I began to fall backwards...and then I woke up, bathed in sweat!

When God starts to tip the dominos on the terrible day of judgment, will you be in that line? Or will you stand aside and be counted with the faithful?

10-104

ARGUING

Titus 3:8-11

(POSB: Note 2, point 1)

Spend Your Time Wisely

How much energy do you waste arguing about the Bible? It is one thing to defend the gospel, quite another to defend your opinion. Listen carefully to this familiar Mother Goose rhyme.

Pussy cat, Pussy cat, where have you been?
I've been to London to visit the queen.
Pussy cat, Pussy cat, what did you there?
I frightened a little mouse under the chair.

Like that cat, Christians sometimes settle for petty involvements, trivial pursuits—chasing mice—when we have the opportunity to spend time with royalty, with the King! [or with His subjects].[1]

Believers should be united in their efforts to reach people for Christ, not wasting time bickering over differences.

---

[1] Craig B. Larson, Editor. *Illustrations for Preaching & Teaching.* (Grand Rapids, MI: Baker Books, 1993), p.267.

PRACTICAL ILLUSTRATIONS

10-105

ASSURANCE

1 Timothy 1:3-11

(POSB: Note 2, point 2)

Assurance Comes Only Through Christ

It was Billy Graham who once stated bluntly, "Being born in America does not make you a Christian any more than being born in a garage makes you a car." In the same sense, being born in a godly family or being born in a Christian hospital does not make you a Christian.

Charles was a young man who was full of life. Raised by Jewish parents, he discovered Christ during his adult years and gave his life to Christ. Charles became quite an evangelist to both the Jew and the Gentile. As he shared his testimony, his words were sharp: "Without Jesus in my life, I would have died and gone to hell."

Interestingly enough, Charles' friend Gary did not have the same belief. Gary had a special love for the Jews. He believed that because the Jews were God's chosen people throughout Old Testament history, they did not need to make a decision for Christ. In essence, they earned a place in heaven because of their "godly heritage," because of their family ties to Abraham and other godly fathers of Israel.

But when another believer asked Gary what would have happened to Charles if he had died before making a decision to accept Christ, Gary's answer was haunting: "I'm not sure where he would have gone."

While people speculate about eternity, heaven is passing them by. Be sure you understand that your entrance into heaven is only through Jesus Christ, not through a godly heritage.

10-106

ASSURANCE

2 Thessalonians 2:10-12

(POSB: Note 4, point 2)

The Joy of Salvation

Without a relationship with God, man is like a fish out of water. Listen to this peculiar story.

Some scientists, according to a story by Harold Bredesen, decided to develop a fish that could live outside of water. So, selecting some healthy red herring, they bred and crossbred, hormoned and chromosomed until they produced a fish that could exist out of water.

But the project director wasn't satisfied. He suspected that though the fish had learned to live on dry land, it still had a secret desire for water.

"Re-educate it," he said. "Change its very desires."

So again they went to work, this time retraining even the strongest reflexes. The result? A fish that would rather die than get wet. Even humidity filled this new fish with dread.

The director, proud of his triumph, took the fish on tour. Well, quite accidentally, according to official reports, it happened—the fish fell into a lake. It sank to the bottom,

PRACTICAL ILLUSTRATIONS

eyes and gills clamped shut, afraid to move, lest it become wetter. And of course it dared not breathe; every instinct said no. Yet breathe it must.

So the fish drew a tentative gill-full. Its eyes bulged. It breathed again and flicked a fin. It breathed a third time and wriggled with delight. Then it darted away. The fish had discovered water.

And with that same wonder, men and women conditioned by a world that rejects God, discover him. For in him we live and move and have our being.[2]

If you've never committed your life to Christ, you are like a fish out of water—you have never really lived! Trust Him...jump in and swim!

❧

10-107

ASSURANCE

2 Thessalonians 2:1-3   **No Fear of Judgment**

(POSB: Note 1, point 1)

As history marches on to a precise beat, the Christian believer needs to keep a Biblical perspective.

A minister, while crossing the Bay of Biscay, became greatly alarmed as he beheld what he thought was an approaching hurricane. Trembling, he addressed himself to one of the sailors: "Do you think she will be able to go through it?" "Through what?" inquired the sailor. "That awful hurricane that is coming down upon us." The old sailor smiled and said: "That storm will never touch us. It has passed us already."

So, in regard to the believer, judgment as to the penalty of our sins is past. We were tried, condemned, and executed in the person of our Surety, Jesus Christ.[3]

If you are a Christian believer, your greatest threat has passed. You can look forward to showers of blessings as you meet with the Savior.

❧

10-108

CALL OF GOD

1 Timothy 1:18-20   **Called to Be God's Warriors**

(POSB: Introduction)

Years ago in the United States, a popular poster featured *Uncle Sam* with his finger pointing to the reader saying, "Uncle Sam Needs You!" With that invitation, Americans left behind homes and careers to become a part of the greatest military force on the face of the earth.

Much preparation went into honing these soldiers and sailors into a fighting machine. The basic training that the raw recruits experienced

---

2 Craig B. Larson, Editor. *Illustrations for Preaching & Teaching*, p.131.

3 *The King's Business.* Walter B. Knight. *3,000 Illustrations for Christian Service.*. (Grand Rapids, MI: Eerdman's Publishing Company, 1971), p.396.

17

turned them from private citizens into powerful commandos, which were then turned loosed on the enemy.

All believers are called to be warriors in this world—warriors for God. But the minister of God is called to do even more: he is called to take charge and to lead in being a warrior.

Have you responded to the call to join God's army? Are you in "battle shape"? Are you fighting the enemy?

❧

10-109

CHOICES

2 Timothy 3:1-9

(POSB: Note 1)

Choose the Path of Life

Scripture leaves no doubt about what is to come—perilous times. The wise man will heed the warning and make the necessary corrections in the course of his life.

> For years, the opening of "The Wide World of Sports" television program illustrated "the agony of defeat" with a painful ending to an attempted ski jump. The skier appeared in good form as he headed down the jump, but then, for no apparent reason, he tumbled head over heels off the side of the jump, bouncing off the supporting structure.
>
> What viewers didn't know was that he chose to fall rather than finish the jump. Why? As he explained later, the jump surface had become too fast, and midway down the ramp, he realized if he completed the jump, he would land on the level ground, beyond the safe sloping landing area, which could have been fatal.
>
> As it was, the skier suffered no more than a headache from the tumble.
>
> To change one's course in life can be a dramatic and sometimes painful undertaking, but change is better than a fatal landing at the end.[4]

As a believer, you must constantly be looking for the dangerous roadblocks and signs that the Lord has told you will surely come. Are you looking ahead or getting caught unaware?

❧

10-110

CHRISTIAN EXAMPLE

1 Thessalonians 1:5-10

(POSB: Introduction)

Be a Good Pattern

Like a dress that is cut and sewn according to a pattern, our lives are patterns—either good or bad—for others to follow. If someone patterned his life after you, what kind of life would be produced? The lines of our lives must be bold enough to see. The instructions on how to live as a Biblical Christian must be included in our pattern. It is very likely that you could be the only Bible that some people ever read.

---

4 Craig B. Larson, Editor. *Illustrations for Preaching & Teaching*, p.21.

PRACTICAL ILLUSTRATIONS

The challenge before you is simply this: Will the pattern of your life produce a beautiful wardrobe of other Christians? Or will those who follow your example become embarrassing "factory seconds" with visible flaws?

The Apostle Paul says that the Thessalonian church was an excellent pattern. He says that they were examples not only to the heathen, but also to believers. Their example is primarily found in their strong conversion and in their thundering forth the Word of the Lord (1 Th.1:8).

❧

10-111

CHRISTIAN LIFE, THE

1 Thessalonians 5:12-28   **Dead to Self, Alive to Christ**

(POSB: Note 4, point 4)

As believers we live in a paradox: we are dead to the world, but alive in Christ.

> The Viet Nam Veteran's Memorial is striking for its simplicity. Etched in a black granite wall are the names of 58,156 Americans who died in that war.
> Since its opening in 1982, the stark monument has stirred deep emotions. Some visitors walk its length slowly, reverently, and without pause. Others stop before certain names, remembering their son or sweetheart or fellow soldier, wiping away tears, tracing the names with their fingers.
> For three Viet Nam veterans—Robert Bedker, Willard Craig, and Darrall Lausch—a visit to the memorial must be especially poignant, for they can walk up to the long ebony wall and find their own names carved in the stone. Because of data-coding errors, each of them was incorrectly listed as killed in action.
> Dead, but alive—a perfect description of the Christian.[5]

Is there evidence in your life that you have died to self and are alive in Christ?

❧

10-112

CHRISTIAN LIFE, THE

Titus 3:1-2   **Impacting Your Culture for Christ**

(POSB: Introduction)

Can you as a Christian believer make a difference in your community? And if so, what difference can you make? Instead of withdrawing from your culture, you are to impact it. After all, you *are* called the salt of the earth (that which preserves) and the light of the world (that which shows the way). Listen for a moment to these ancient words that contrast the Christian faith with other false religions.

> Christians are not differentiated from other people by country, language, or customs; you see, they do not live in cities of their own, or speak some strange

---

[5] Craig B. Larson, Editor. *Illustrations for Preaching & Teaching*, p.47.

PRACTICAL ILLUSTRATIONS

dialect....They follow local customs in clothing, food, and the other aspects of life. But at the same time, they demonstrate to us the unusual form of their own citizenship.

They live in their own native lands, but as aliens....They marry and have children just like everyone else, but they do not kill unwanted babies. They offer a shared table, but not a shared bed....They obey the appointed laws and go beyond the laws in their own lives.

· They love everyone, but are persecuted by all. They are put to death and gain life. They are poor and yet make many rich....They are marked and bless in return. They are treated outrageously and behave respectfully to others.

When they do good, they are punished as evildoers; when punished, they rejoice as if being given new life. They are attacked...as aliens and are persecuted by....[the world]; yet those who hate them cannot give any reason for their hostility.[6]

Usually the believer can do little about how authorities in government conduct their affairs, but the believer can do a great deal about his behavior as a citizen within the state.

◈

10-113

CHRISTIAN LIFE, THE

1 Timothy 3:14-16   **Knowing the Way to Heaven**

(POSB: Note 1)

It should never be assumed that fallen man will naturally gravitate upwards. The Christian believer needs constant reminders to learn how to behave as a Christian should.

When the jumble around the starting line of a certain yacht race cleared, the helmsman of the leading yacht remarked rather uneasily, "I never expected to find myself in the lead." He made the same remark several times, but his crew told him it was nothing to complain about. As they rounded the first mark, well ahead, he said, "I think we'll have to let [the] boat [behind] pass us." "No we'll not," said the crew, "we're doing fine." "The trouble is," said the helmsman, "that I don't know where to go next. I was so sure there would be other boats in front that I didn't take the trouble to study the course."

There are too many Christians who will have a poor place in heaven because they are living their Christian lives like this helmsman. They were meant to be conquerors, but the last shall be first and the first last because they did not study to show themselves approved unto God—workmen that need not be ashamed.[7]

If you want to know how to behave in the church, the place to begin is in the Word of God. Are you a good student of Scripture, or have you merely been following the crowd?

◈

---

6   Craig B. Larson, Editor. *Illustrations for Preaching & Teaching.* From the *Letter to Diognetus*, p.28.
7   Donald Grey Barnhouse. *Let Me Illustrate.* (Grand Rapids, MI: Fleming H. Revell, 1967), p.47.

PRACTICAL ILLUSTRATIONS

10-114

CHRISTIAN LIFE, THE

Titus 3:8-11   **Obeying God's Instructions**

(POSB: Introduction)

In order to legally drive a car, you must first do two important things.

- Take a written test on the rules of the road.
- Apply the written rules to the open road, driving with an examiner by your side.

The role of the examiner is to see how well you apply what you know in a real life experience. Many of us know the rules but do not get our driver's license because of the most important test—the driving test.

The Christian life can be compared to taking a driving test. Most of us know some things about the Bible and the Christian life, but we have a hard time passing the actual test of living the Christian life. Many a believer has lost control and run off the proper course because he did not apply what he knew to real life experiences. What is the answer to improving our spiritual driving? It is to learn then obey what God reveals to us in His Word.

10-115

CHURCH

1 Thessalonians 1:1-4   **Built upon a Solid Rock**

(POSB: Note 3)

Only the church of Jesus Christ will stand when the storms of trouble come. An organization might look like a church, act like a church, and talk like a church; but if the foundation is faulty, it will fall apart.

Years ago, a pastor veered off course and built his own church kingdom. He had no trouble finding people to finance his ego as he attempted to build a ministry, hoping to become internationally famous. When the decision was made to build a large sanctuary, he decided to forgo the skills of a professional building contractor in order to save funds. The decision was made to solicit volunteers from among church members.

By experience, we all know that if a person takes unwise short cuts, he will pay for them later. As time went by, this ministry began to crack at the seams. The minister's lack of integrity caused him to self-destruct. Ironically, as his ministry was cracking, his beautiful building began to crack as well. In the center of the building, the floor cracked from one end to the other.

What kind of lesson can we draw from this example? A church and a Christian will crack if they are not built upon a firm foundation, not trusting Christ. As the great hymn-writer Edward Mote reminds us...

> My hope is built on nothing less
> Than Jesus' blood and righteousness;
> I dare not trust the sweetest frame,

But wholly lean on Jesus' name.
On Christ, the solid Rock, I stand—
All other ground is sinking sand,
All other ground is sinking sand.[8]

10-116

CHURCH

1 Timothy 3:14-16

Evaluating Your Priorities

(POSB: Introduction)

If the Apostle Paul were caught in a time warp from the first century and found himself in your church, would he recognize anything familiar? Allow your imagination to wander into this possible conversation as you lead Paul on a tour of your church:

"Paul, on behalf of all of the Christians from our era, we would like to welcome you to the modern, all-improved church. As you walk around, what do you think so far? Do our numbers impress you? How about the size of our facility? Have you had a chance to browse through our information brochure? It will tell you all about the many programs we offer the people of our community."

Waiting to take a long bow for our accomplishments, we were somewhat disturbed by Paul's response. "In the churches of my time," Paul said, "we spent time building relationships in order to really know each other. Our meeting place was from house to house. And our programs, as you call them, were pretty simplified: Love God. Love one another. Love the lost." "Oh" we sighed in embarrassment.

God is not concerned with how big or pretty your church is, how many programs you have, or how fancy your website is. God cares about the behavior of believers and relationships within the church. Would He be pleased with *your* church?

10-117

CHURCH

1 Timothy 3:14-16

Filling in the Gap

(POSB: Note 2, point 2)

The Scriptures clearly teach us that "every joint supplies." That being true, when one part of the body is missing, there is a gap. Listen to this striking story set in rural Europe.

A traveler in a European village discovered a beautiful custom. At night she saw the people going to the church, each carrying a little bronze lamp. These lamps [were] placed in sockets by their pews. The soft light of the lamps was the only illumination for the service. If a member was absent, there was a dark space!

---

8 Public Domain.

PRACTICAL ILLUSTRATIONS

We do not carry lamps to church, but we do send forth light. When we are absent there is darkness in our stead. The more people at church, the greater the inspiration. Many small lamps together make a great and beautiful light.

The first Christian church in Jerusalem had no building. It had a small membership; it had no officers; it had no pastor; it had no choir or pipe organ; it had no wealth; and, most startling of all, it had no New Testament.

What made it a successful church? Just this: It had the total attendance of its membership. Pentecost was possible because they were *all* together in one place.[9]

God invites you to regularly share your light with His body, the church, to be a faithful family member in your church. Are you part of the great and beautiful light, or is there too often darkness in your place where your light should be shining?

❧

10-118

CHURCH

I Thessalonians 1:1-4   **Serving on the Front Lines**

(POSB: Note 2)

It is God's will that every member of a church participate in its ministry. Unfortunately, some have sought out the "good seats in the back" to watch the other members do all the work. Author Frank Tillapaugh points this out with the following story:

At a Navigator conference years ago the main speaker referred to what he termed "front-line" and "rear-echelon" ministries. As a combat veteran he had vivid memories of the difference in attitude between those directly joined in battle on the front lines and those indirectly involved a few miles behind in the rear echelon.

The guys on the front lines didn't complain much. They were too busy fighting the enemy. Camaraderie was built quickly. People had to work together; it was a matter of life and death. They took their objectives and strategy seriously—successful execution was imperative. Little things, such as how good the food tasted, didn't matter significantly. What did matter was that they were still alive to eat it.

Once you went a few miles behind the front, however, attitudes changed drastically. Back there, griping was a way of life. Men complained about everything—the food, the weather, the officers. Something was wrong with everyone and everything.[10]

In any church, there are all kinds of people...
* those on the front lines
* those who will only participate reluctantly
* those who stay in the back or on the sidelines
* those who are in full retreat

A model church strives to get as many as possible on the front line. Where are you?

❧

---

[9] Selected from *Rev. Ralph V. Gilbert in Southern Churchmen.* Walter B. Knight. *3,000 Illustrations for Christian Service*, p.135.

[10] Frank R. Tillapaugh. *Unleashing the Church.* (Ventura, CA: Regal Books, 1982), pp.122-123.

PRACTICAL ILLUSTRATIONS

10-119

COMMITMENT
Philemon 22-25
(POSB: Note 6)

Giving All to Christ

Giving all to Christ is no light matter. It means to give Jesus Christ everything that you are and have in this world.

> The story is told of a gospel crusade in a third world country where great numbers of people were responding to the call of Christ. One night the altar call was for the effort of world missions. The evangelist said, "We need to send missionaries to other countries. What can you give for the cause?" The altar was filled with people who brought money and other precious possessions. As people streamed to the altar, one woman was crying and pushing her way to the altar. Through her sobs, she threw herself to the altar and told the evangelist, "I'm a poor woman. The only thing I can give is my life!"

This poor woman had discovered the secret of giving all in order to follow Christ. He does not want your money or your talents. He just wants you...all of you. If He has you, then He has all you have.

10-120

COMMITMENT
Titus 3:12-15
(POSB: Introduction)

Making Vows of Integrity

One of the most impressive parts of a wedding service is when the bride and groom exchange their vows, agreeing to love each other "until death do us part." Is that kind of vow to be taken seriously in today's culture? Yes. God expects us to honor our vows to each other. Promises are not made to be broken; they are made to be kept—even when it is inconvenient to us.

> Robertson McQuilkin made such a vow to his wife Muriel. The circumstances of life had been very good to the McQuilkin's. After a fruitful time as a missionary to Japan, McQuilkin accepted a call to become president of Columbia Bible College and Seminary. Under his leadership, the school grew and became very successful. At the pinnacle of success, McQuilkin resigned at the age of 57. He stepped down to care for Muriel who had contracted Alzheimer's—an incurable disease. Much of the Christian world was in shock. How could this man who could do so much for so many quit his job, leave his ministry? Unmoved by pleas to reconsider his decision, McQuilkin stated that he had promised to care for his wife in sickness and in health..."until death do us part." It was integrity that moved McQuilkin to pledge his love to his wife when they were first married. It was that same integrity that caused him to remain committed to those vows.

How committed are you? Commitment is seen in anyone who does not allow circumstances to frustrate and annul a promise that has been made to others or to God. Believers should stand as dynamic examples of what commitment is all about.

PRACTICAL ILLUSTRATIONS

10-121

COMMUNICATION

1 Timothy 2:9-15

(*POSB: Note 2*)

Learning How to Listen

It is almost impossible to talk and listen at the same time. If we do most of the talking, we cannot hear God speaking to us. In *When I Relax I Feel Guilty*, author Tim Hansel notes:

> An American Indian was in downtown New York, walking with his friend who lived in New York City. Suddenly he said, "I hear a cricket."
> "Oh, you're crazy," his friend replied.
> "No, I hear a cricket. I do! I'm sure of it."
> "It's the noon hour. There are people bustling around, cars honking, taxis squealing, noises from the city. I'm sure you can't hear it."
> "I'm sure I do." He listened attentively and then walked to the corner, across the street, and looked all around. Finally on the corner he found a shrub in a large cement planter. He dug beneath the leaves and found a cricket. His friend was astounded. But the Cherokee said, "No. My ears are no different from yours. It simply depends on what you are listening to. Here, let me show you." He reached into his pocket and pulled out a handful of change....And he dropped it on the concrete. Every head within a block turned. "You see what I mean?" he said as he began picking up his coins. "It all depends on what you are listening for."[11]

In a church filled with a variety of sounds, the truth rings clear when we close our mouths and train our ears to listen for God's Word.

10-122

CONSCIENCE

1 Timothy 1:18-20

(*POSB: Note 3*)

The Foolishness of Ignoring Your Conscience

What happens to a person who puts away his conscience? According to Scripture, his faith can be shipwrecked. Ignoring his conscience will cause him to drift farther and farther off course. Destruction awaits. A person must pay attention to the instruction God provides in His Word. In *Returning to Your First Love*, Pastor Tony Evans writes:

> I'll never forget the time my younger brother rebelled against my father. He didn't like my father's rules....Now, little brother was the...wrestling champion....At 250 pounds, he was big and strong....
> My father told my brother to do something...but my brother didn't think he should have to do it. So he frowned, shook his head, and said, "No!"
> Dad said, "Oh yes!"
> Little brother said, "No!"

---

[11] Craig B. Larson, Editor. *Illustrations for Preaching & Teaching*, p. 240.

PRACTICAL ILLUSTRATIONS

My father...took him upstairs, and helped him pack his suitcase. My brother jumped [at the opportunity] and said, "Yeah, I'm leaving! I don't' have to take this!"

And he walked out of the house. But he forgot a few things. He forgot he didn't have a job. He forgot it was snowing outside. He forgot he didn't have a car. He jumped [at the opportunity], but he forgot that when you don't have anything, you don't jump.

So twenty minutes later...knock, knock! Brother was at the door wanting to come home. My father delivered him to the elements that he might be taught respect....

When he was put out, my brother was no longer under the protective custody of our home. He had to fend for himself. [12]

Ignoring your conscience leaves you out in the cold, fending for yourself instead of being under the protection of God and in the safe haven of a family of believers.

10-123

<small>CONSCIENCE</small>
1 Timothy 1:18-20
(POSB: Deeper Study #1)

The Need for Conviction

Most of us can relate to being caught with our hand in the cookie jar and the guilt that comes along with it.

A little ten-year old boy learned this valuable lesson early in life. It seems the "cool" thing to do was to go to the school store and slip pencils and pens into your pocket without getting caught. So after successfully pocketing several items, the boy thought to himself, "This is too easy. Today the pencils—tomorrow...who knows?"

Soon, word came through the grapevine that any student caught stealing would be harshly punished. In this little boy's mind, the punishment was translated into the horrible thought that Mom and Dad would find out.

Panic-stricken, the little boy felt both scared and sorry. Under his breath, he prayed this simple prayer: "God, if I get out of this, I'll never steal anything ever again." Later, as the "cool" kids headed off to the store after class, he went the opposite direction to rid himself of the stolen supplies.

This little boy grew up to become a solid citizen, but he still regretted one thing: he did not return the stolen items. He just threw them away.

Thankfully, when your conscience convicts you of sin, God does not throw you away. Instead, He redeems all those who ask for forgiveness.

---

12 Craig B. Larson. *Choice Contemporary Stories & Illustrations.* (Grand Rapids, MI: Baker Books, 1998), #58.

PRACTICAL ILLUSTRATIONS

10-124

CONVERSATION

2 Timothy 2:14-21

(POSB: Introduction)

The Danger of Evil Words

Have you ever thought about how powerful words can be? History warns us that words have been the sparks that have ignited horrible wars. Broken relationships haunt us because words cannot be taken back.

How much verbal abuse can a person take before losing his temper? Think about it. When others speak ill or evil about you, how much can you take before you explode in hurt and anger? On the other hand, consider every unkind or evil word you have ever spoken or thought about another person. Imagine a scar on the heart of every individual who has been the target of your thoughtless or cruel words. A time will come when there is no more room for healing. Hurt feelings, damaged relationships, broken homes, and even crimes have resulted from carelessly spoken words. It is a fact that more trouble is brewed and stirred by words than by any other act.

10-125

CONVERSATION

2 Timothy 4:1-5

(POSB: Note 1)

Drawing on God's Strength

When you share the Word of God with others, do you ever feel you are out on a limb all by yourself? Take heart, for God is not only watching you, He is also there to help you.

Dan, a new believer, was looking forward to an upcoming class reunion. Some of his old classmates who had been close friends had since moved up the corporate ladder of success.

As the day grew nearer, Dan began to feel a twinge of nerves. "What can I say to these fellows who were such close friends? One of them is now a scientist. Another is a university professor. Still another is a great scholar and writer. What can I say that will lead them to Christ?"

Looking for encouragement, Dan called the man who had led him to Christ. "Mike, what shall I do? It's too late for me to back out now." Upon hearing Dan's concern, Mike graciously offered his advice. "Dan, there is no need for you to feel intimidated. It is your *responsibility* to reveal God's Word. If you will share the gospel, the Lord will help you and cause your sharing to bear fruit. Trust Him. Draw on His strength."

The believer must never share the gospel in his own strength. God and Christ are watching our efforts: they are with us, will even give us the opportunity and the words to say. If we will be faithful to share the *good news*, the Lord will bless our efforts.

PRACTICAL ILLUSTRATIONS

10-126

CONVERSATION

2 Timothy 2:14-21

(POSB: Note 3)

Put Away Godless Chatter

Kids have been known to say the cutest things. Sometimes their mis-pronunciation of a word will actually bring a clearer meaning. Here is an example.

> A four-year old boy decided that he'd make an attempt at reciting the prayer which he had heard in church. "And forgive us our trash baskets," he asked, "as we forgive those who trash basket against us."[13]

Enough said? Godless chatter belongs in the trash basket!

10-127

CONVERSATION

2 Timothy 2:14-21

(POSB: Note 1)

Weigh Your Words

A person's words will influence others—either for good or for bad. Therefore, as believers, we must not allow ourselves to become entangled in useless arguments and petty discussions about God's Word and the gospel message. We are not called to lift up our intelligence and show our pride; we are called to lift up Christ and show others the cross.

> Calvin Coolidge wisely expressed it, "One of the first lessons a president has to learn is that every word he says weighs a ton."[14]

Likewise, as believers, we must weigh every word we say in light of eternity—our own as well as others'!

10-128

CONVERSION

1 Timothy 3:1-7

(POSB: Note 4)

The Critical Need for Discipleship

A saying that is far too often true is this: more than one spiritual neck has been broken by falling off the platform. How often a new convert is paraded across the platform as a "super" conversion. Here is one example:

> Al was a successful businessman and middle-aged convert. He had a unique way with words and quickly became the featured speaker at Christian meetings. Less than five years after conversion he became an elder in his church—a position that simply

---

13 Paul Lee Tan. *Encyclopedia of 7,700 Illustrations: Signs of the Times.* (Rockville, MD: Assurance Publishers, 1985), p.527.

14 G. Curtis Jones. *1000 Illustrations for Preaching and Teaching.* (Nashville, TN: Broadman & Holman Publishers, 1986), p.305.

overwhelmed him. He was much more content to be a featured speaker around town than to have to adhere to his biblical responsibilities as an elder. It did not take long for him to burn out and backslide. His previous joy turned into a haunting journey.

Al's life is a lesson for all believers. If discipleship is omitted, then failure is not far behind.

᎒

10-129

CORRUPTION

1 Timothy 6:3-5
(POSB: Note 4)

Corruption of the Mind

It is sad to say, but our culture has been infected with an epidemic of mental corruption. For example...

Ron was a popular university professor whose favorite pastime was confusing Christians in his philosophy class. The course was advertised in the college catalog as "Understanding the New Testament," but it was renamed by believing Christians who took the course as "*Misunderstanding* the New Testament."

His twisting of the Scriptures would have been a little more bearable if he were simply a practicing pagan. But the tragedy was compounded because he was an ordained minister. Under the guise of the cloth, he spoke as one who had authority on two levels: both the academic and the spiritual.

One semester Ron met his match. Two Christian students refused to follow the path of deception and confusion. Ron's aggressive and confrontational teaching style drove these two Christians into an even deeper relationship with the Lord. With each point of deception, they went right to God's Word, and in a kind and gracious spirit, they corrected the professor.

Did Ron cave in and see things their way? No, but note what happened: other Christian students who were teetering on the fence jumped off and landed on a firmer faith because of the witness of their two classmates.

᎒

10-130

COUNTERFEIT

1 Timothy 6:3-5
(POSB: Introduction)

No Excuse for Ignorance

How can you tell if someone is a phony or a counterfeit? Simply put, when he fails to tell the truth. But what is the truth and where is it found? The Christian believer's best guard against falsehood is knowing for himself what the Bible says. With God's Word available, there is no excuse for ignorance. Ignorance is like a welcome mat at the door inviting the wolf to come in to destroy God's precious lambs.

᎒

PRACTICAL ILLUSTRATIONS

10-131

DEACON

1 Timothy 3:8-13

(POSB: Introduction)

The Need for Spirit-filled Deacons

What if this announcement appeared in your church newsletter?

ANNOUNCEMENT

It has come to the attention of the church leaders that many of our members feel their needs are being neglected. In order to care for these members, the leadership has approved the position of deacon. The candidate who fills this position must have:

- a great personality
- a college education
- a 15-passenger van

For more information about the requirements for this position, contact I. M. Kidding.

Certainly, this "announcement" would never appear in your church newsletter. Deacons are not appointed to serve on the basis of worldly qualifications but on the basis of servant hood—helping and relieving the minister within the church. Deacons are appointed to serve selflessly and to teach others how to serve with them. Therefore, a local church with Spirit-filled deacons is an essential if the life of Jesus Christ is to be seen in the community.

≈∂

10-132

DEATH

2 Timothy 4:6-8

(POSB: Note 1)

Are You Willing to Die for Christ?

Jesus Christ died for the world. But more important, Jesus Christ died for you. In a single act on the cross, Jesus paid your debt for sin. He would never ask anyone to do anything that He had not done first. He died for you. Will you die for Him?

In "Planet in Rebellion," George Vandeman wrote: "It was May 21, 1946. The place—Los Alamos. A young and daring scientist was carrying out a necessary experiment in preparation for the atomic test to be conducted in the waters of the South Pacific....He had successfully performed such an experiment many times before. In his effort to determine the amount of U-235 necessary for a chain reaction—scientists call it the critical mass—he would push two hemispheres of uranium together. Then, just as the mass became critical, he would push them apart with his screwdriver, thus instantly stopping the chain reaction.

"But that day, just as the material became critical, the screwdriver slipped! The hemispheres of uranium came too close together. Instantly the room was filled with a dazzling bluish haze. Young Louis Slotin, instead of ducking and thereby possibly saving himself, tore the two hemispheres apart with his hands and thus interrupted the chain reaction. By this instant...he saved the lives of the seven other persons in the room....As he waited...for the car that was to take them to the hospital, he said quietly to his companion, 'You'll come through all right. But I haven't the faintest chance myself.' It was only too true. Nine days later he died in agony. Nineteen centuries ago the Son of the living God walked directly into sin's most concentrated radiation, allowed himself to be touched by its curse, and let it take his life....But by that act he broke the chain reaction. He broke the power of sin."[15]

You will only die once. But *how* you die, *why* you die, and *who* you die for is something every believer needs to think about while there is still time.

❧

10-133

DECEPTION

2 Thessalonians 2:4-9
(POSB: Note 5)

Are You a "Sucker" or a "Saint"?

P.T. Barnum is credited with the saying, "There's a sucker born every minute." His point is well taken, for mankind is prone to look for the quick fix and is amused by the spectacular. Satan is the ultimate craftsman of illusion.

Duveen, the famous English art connoisseur, took his little daughter to the beach one day, but she would not go into the chilly water. After persuasion failed, Duveen borrowed a tea-kettle, built a fire, heated a little water until it steamed beautifully; then, with a great flourish, he poured it into the ocean. His greatly impressed daughter went in without a murmur.

Where can we find a better example of one of Satan's tricks? He dilutes an ocean of unbelief with a steaming teakettle of Christian ethics and people go wading in, self-satisfied but unaware that they are bathing in unbelief.[16]

By definition, a sucker is someone who is gullible and gets pulled into an unhealthy situation. A saint is someone who is pulled to the cross, a place where deception is exposed and the truth is clear to see. Are you living like a sucker or like a saint?

❧

10-134

DECEPTION

2 Timothy 3:1-9
(POSB: Note 4, point 1)

Avoiding Deception

Do you think for a moment that a wolf will attack the strongest sheep in the herd? Of course not. He will shadow the herd and seek out the sheep that is sick or that has gone astray. And it is not just the four-legged wolves that we need to be aware of. Their two-legged cousins are just as cunning.

---

[15] Craig B. Larson. *Illustrations for Preaching & Teaching*, p. 48.
[16] Donald Grey Barnhouse. *Let Me Illustrate*, pp.280-281.

PRACTICAL ILLUSTRATIONS

Coming home from work, a woman stopped at the corner deli to buy a chicken for supper. The butcher reached into a barrel, grabbed the last chicken he had, flung it on the scales behind the counter, and told the woman its weight.

She thought for a moment. "I really need a bit more chicken than that," she said. "Do you have any larger ones?"

Without a word, the butcher put the chicken back into the barrel, groped around as though finding another, pulled the same chicken out, and placed it on the scales. "This chicken weighs one pound more," he announced.

The woman pondered her options and then said, "Okay. I'll take them both."[17]

This woman foiled the butcher, but how many others had he tricked before her? The marketplace of life is full of imposters who scan the crowd for the gullible. In every area of life, make sure the individual you are following is not leading you astray! Take the time to ponder your options.

10-135

DECEPTION

2 Thessalonians 2:10-12

(POSB: Note 2)

The Danger of Deception

It is a very dangerous thing to ignore the truth. Yet time and again, men plow ahead to do what they want to do. Listen to this very graphic example of men who ignored the truth.

Many years ago, when the Egyptian troops first conquered Nubia, a regiment was crossing a desert. The heat was oppressive, almost beyond endurance; the supply of water nearly exhausted. Far in the horizon they seemed to see a beautiful lake bordered with palm-trees.

The Arab guide, who well understood the desert wastes, told the soldiers there was no lake there, that what they saw was only a mirage, a floating delusion on the sky. But the thirsty soldiers saw something which they believed to be water, and were determined to trust their sight rather than his words. They insisted upon their guide leading them to the water.

He protested, and resisted even to death. When they had killed him, the whole regiment, wild with excitement and eager for the cooling waters, left the course indicated by their guide and started for the lake. On and on they pressed over the burning sands; hour after hour they endured the heat, hoping to gain the refreshing waters of the lake, but that object fled before them like a phantom. Self-deceived, exhausted by the heat, and overcome with fatigue, they began to fall upon the burning sands and die. They all perished.

---

[17] Clark Cothern. Tecumseh, Michigan. Quoted in *Leadership Journal.* (Carol Stream, IL: Christianity Today), Fall 1994, p.43.

Long after, the Arabs in search found the body of the guide, a martyr to his faithfulness, while the bodies of the soldiers were found far out upon the wild wastes, where they fell in their vain search to find water where there was none. Their sincerity did not save them from death (as told by Sir S.W. Baker).[18]

The followers of the antichrist might be sincere, but because of their rejection of the truth, they will be sincerely wrong, paying the ultimate price for their rejection.

❧

10-136

DECEPTION

1 Timothy 4:1-5

(POSB: Note 1)

Satan's Sinister Schemes

There is a web of conspiracy that has been inspired by the devil. He has no problem finding willing individuals to do his bidding. The scary thing is that his volunteers look a lot like the real thing, the teachers of truth!

The story has been told of a conversation between two fallen angels. "Trickster" and "Tempter" returned to their demonic den after another day of destroying people's lives. Sitting at the table, they began to compare their dastardly notes. "What did you do today?" sneered Tempter. With an evil grin, Trickster spoke in arrogant breaths. "I've had a great day. Several of my projects are finally beginning to bear fruit. Today a pastor made the decision to rationalize the miracles in the Bible. A seminary professor has agreed with our master's agenda and is willing to recruit students to worship anyone but Christ. A Sunday school teacher has turned in his teacher's book and has decided to replace the study of the Bible with an 'issues' class."

"Why, that's nothing compared to what I've done today!" responded Tempter. "I've convinced the choir director to cut down on worshipful music and to use popular music instead to appeal to a broader crowd. And he has found a verse in the Bible to justify what he is doing. I've also been at work in the heart of the pastor of another church. I've convinced him that he is the reason for the success of the church and that he can take the church anywhere he wants to go. He is going to be a wonderful pawn in our hands."

All of a sudden the door blew open and Satan stood basking in his evil light. "I overheard what you have done. But that is not enough! Get back to work...NOW!"

Satan stays busy placing false teachers into key places of influence. He never lets up in his war of deception. Neither can we let up in carrying forth the truth.

❧

[18] Elon Foster, Editor. *6,000 Classic Sermon Illustrations.* (Grand Rapids, MI: Baker Book House, 1992), pp.232-233.

33

Practical Illustrations

10-137

DETERMINATION

1 Timothy 6:11-16

(POSB: Note 3)

Focus on the Finish

Many distractions seek to pull you as a Christian believer off course. But you are in a race—the race of your life—and the question is, how will you run?

On March 6, 1987, Eamon Coughlan, the Irish world record holder at 1500 meters, was running in a qualifying heat at the World Indoor Track Championships in Indianapolis. With two and a half laps left, he was tripped. He fell, but he got up and with great effort managed to catch the leaders. With only 20 yards left in the race, he was in third place—good enough to qualify for the finals.

He looked over his shoulder to the inside, and, seeing no one, he let up. But another runner, charging hard on the outside, passed Coughlan a yard before the finish, thus eliminating him from the finals. Coughlan's great comeback effort was rendered worthless by taking his eyes off the finish line.[19]

Are you concentrating on the finish line, eternal life? Or are you giving up before the race of life is over?

10-138

DISCERNMENT

1 Timothy 6:17-21

(POSB: Note 2, point 2)

Are You Listening Clearly?

It is critical that anyone who speaks for Jesus Christ be listened to clearly—and with discernment. Listen closely to this example.

The setting was a Bible conference where a variety of speakers were invited to address the participants. One of the speakers was a man noted for his deep scholarship and quick wit. Popular across the country as a Christian keynote speaker, his address shocked the people who heard him. His opinion was that God had changed His mind about a few things since the Bible was written thousands of years ago. For example...

- Certain sins are really not a problem anymore. After all, our cultural values have been up-dated.
- Homosexuality is simply an issue of sexual preference.
- There are errors in the Bible. We need an inner-guide to show us what is true and to understand the wisdom of the great writers down through the ages.

---

[19] Craig B. Larson, Editor. *Illustrations for Preaching & Teaching*, p.178.

PRACTICAL ILLUSTRATIONS

One by one, people began to whisper. "Did you hear what I heard?" "What should we do?" "Would it be rude to get up and leave?" "Do you think he could be right? After all, he is a respected authority on the Bible." Before long, the brave ones began to close their notebooks and make their way to the exits. But many more sat in their seats, soaking up the deception of the false teacher.

How clearly are you listening to the messenger of the gospel?

10-139

DISCIPLESHIP

2 Timothy 1:1-5

(POSB: Note 2)

Making the Most of Every Opportunity

What would you do if God sent a young man like Timothy into your life? Would you be prepared to train him? Hopefully more so than this man!

Ernie had been a hard worker all his life. Close to retirement, he wanted to just *coast on in,* that is, not get involved, not create waves, and get the job done with the least amount of resistance. His experience was, if you wanted something done (and done right), just do it yourself. True, it added more of a burden to his schedule, but at least he could go to bed at night knowing that the job had been done right.

Unfortunately, this mindset affected Ernie's ability to teach and train younger men on the job. One young man in particular approached Ernie and said, "This is all new to me. Would you help me until I can learn the ropes?" The young worker's expectations were pretty simple: Have the older man work side by side with him, teaching what his years of experience had taught him. But Ernie's ideas were not even close. They rode together to the fitness center occasionally, had an occasional fast-food meal together, and talked about the latest headlines from yesterday's sports page.

When they finally went their separate ways, what had the young worker learned from Ernie? How to get to the fitness center, how to avoid the greasiest french-fries, and how to figure batting averages in his head.

What did Ernie get out of the training period? Nothing but a lost opportunity to pass on the trade he had mastered through the years—and the chance to assure that quality work would be carried on in his absence. Both Ernie and the young worker lost out in every way: in time, training, and a friendship that could have been lasting between teacher and student.

God places people in your life for a reason. Make sure you are not losing the opportunity to teach and train them!

PRACTICAL ILLUSTRATIONS

10-140

DISCIPLESHIP

1 Timothy 1:1-2

(POSB: Introduction)

Producing Disciples for Christ

What have you done in the past five years that will have lasting value? Sometimes we can get so caught up in *doing* that we forget *what* we are supposed to do. If you were employed by a store that sold power-tools to craftsmen, you would want to sell tools that would benefit your customers, something that would help them produce their finest work. You would be wasting your time and theirs if you tried to sell them something inferior or something they would not use.

Strange as it may seem, many Christians are busy doing everything except what they are called to do, that is, make disciples. The challenge from Scripture is to stop getting sidetracked and get busy doing the Lord's work. Start producing disciples for Christ. A disciple made in Jesus' name will produce lasting results. Like the excellent craftsman, the believer needs to have the correct tools in order to produce a quality disciple. Nothing else will do.

One thing that is desperately needed in the church is the vital ministry of making disciples, of nourishing and nurturing men and women as sons and daughters of the faith. In seeing the relationship that existed between the Apostle Paul and Timothy, we should be challenged more and more to make disciples—to get to the task of growing leaders within God's church.

10-141

DISCIPLINE

1 Timothy 5:17-20

(POSB: Note 2)

The Need for Proper Discipline

The Christian believer has a very sober charge to make certain that an elder receives the protection or discipline that Scripture demands. Here is one story that shows the right way to bring discipline to an elder.

Bruce was the minister of an independent church whose past finally caught up with him. For years, he was able to cover his illicit sexual excursions. Those on his staff went out of their way to defend his reputation in the community. They believed the church's business did not belong in the tabloids. The church's business belonged in the church.

At first, Len, his associate pastor, came to him in confidence and told him of the news he was hearing. He pleaded for the sake of Christ for Bruce to turn from his immoral affairs. But instead of thanking his associate for his concern, Bruce lashed out at Len and said, "You have no right to judge me. Furthermore, if my sex-life becomes public, this church and your position will go down the tubes. It would be best for you to be quiet...or else."

Because Len was a man of integrity, he refused to be intimidated by Bruce's threat. His next step was to assemble the other staff ministers and meet with Bruce once more. All of these ministers loved Bruce and wanted to protect his reputation. They offered him confidentiality and restoration. They wanted him to take a sabbatical and fdget some counseling. But, again, instead of being grateful for their offer of grace, Bruce verbally attacked them all.

Refusing to repent, Bruce saw his staff resign one by one. As the church began to sink in the icy waters of gossip and rumor, Len finally submitted his resignation. Less that a year later, the church dissolved and Bruce lost his ministry.

Scriptural discipline has never been popular in the church, but withholding it will create a church perverted by sin. The alternative? A church living according to the principles of Scripture and perfected in holiness.

10-142

DOCTRINE

1 Timothy 4:1-5   **Selfless or Selfish?**

(POSB: Note 3)

To be self-sacrificing sounds very religious. But the real test is found in who or what is being glorified or honored. Is it selfless or selfish? Listen to Aesop's Fable, *The Mouse and the Frog*.

On an ill-fated day a mouse made the acquaintance of a frog, and they set off on their travels together. The frog pretended to be very fond of the mouse and invited him to visit the pond in which he lived. To keep his companion out of harm's way, the frog tied the mouse's front foot to his own hind leg, and thus they proceeded for some distance by land. When they came to the pond, the frog told the mouse to trust him and be brave as he began swimming across the water. But, no sooner had they reached the middle of the pond than the frog suddenly plunged to the bottom, dragging the unfortunate mouse after him. Now the struggling and floundering mouse made such a great commotion in the water that he managed to attract the attention of a hawk, who pounced upon the mouse and carried him away to be devoured. Since the frog was still tied to the mouse, he shared the same fate of his companion and was justly punished for his treachery.

Beware of false teachers who pretend to look out for your good. When they reap what they sow, you do not want to be part of the harvest!

10-143

DUTY

1 Timothy 5:21-25   **The Danger of Being Partial**

(POSB: Introduction)

As believers we must do our duty—no matter what the circumstance. American history gives us a stirring and powerful example of objectivity under stressful conditions, as seen in the movie *Gods and Generals*.

PRACTICAL ILLUSTRATIONS

During the Civil War, three deserters from the Southern armies were captured in Virginia. The adjutant to General Thomas "Stonewall" Jackson reported the capture. Worse yet was the news that the deserters were from Jackson's own brigade.

Without hesitation, the general ordered that they were to be tried for their crimes and, if found guilty, to be executed. The younger commander hesitated, but Jackson explained that soldiers cannot choose when to be in the army and when to go their own way. He further instructed his lesser experienced adjutant that the rest of the army depends on the faithful, unswerving, impartial service of every member. The general went on to instruct, "Duty is ours; the consequences are God's."[20]

We are in a spiritual battle, a battle for our lives. The rules do not change with our whims and pleasures. We must serve God without partiality.

10-144

ELECTION

1 Thessalonians 1:1-4

(POSB: Note 7)

God's Arrow of Grace

We cannot escape the wonderful truth that God chose us. Once He calls a person, life can never be the same again.

Cartoonist Hank Ketcham's Dennis the Menace was seen talking to his little buddy, Joey, about Cupid.

"And if he shoots you with an arrow, you fall in love whether you want to or not."
Well, God is certainly not cupid. But from a bow that strongly resembles a cross, the arrow of His grace has been shot right at humanity. In fact, His love is eternal; and when it hits someone in the heart, the only possible response is to fall in love with Him.

Has His arrow pierced your heart?

10-145

ENCOURAGEMENT

1 Thessalonians 2:1-12

(POSB: Note 11)

Encouraging Our Leaders

Believers are to be in the business of edification. For certain, this will not come from the world. It must come through the church.

In his book *Wind and Fire*, Bruce Larson points out some interesting facts about leadership and sand hill cranes:

---

[20] *Gods and Generals.* Warner Bros., 2003.

These large birds, who fly great distances across continents, have three remarkable qualities. First, they rotate leadership. No one bird stays out in front all the time. Second, they choose leaders who can handle turbulence. And then, all during the time one bird is leading, the rest are honking their affirmation. That's not a bad model for the church. Certainly we need leaders who can handle turbulence and who are aware that leadership ought to be shared. But most of all, we need a church where we are all honking encouragement.[21]

10-146

ENCOURAGEMENT
1 Thessalonians 5:4-11
(POSB: Note 4)

Helping Others Along the Way

Every true believer is going to heaven. Meanwhile, until Christ calls us home, we have plenty of work to do in this world. A great part of that work is to comfort and encourage one another.

In the fall of the year, Linda, a young woman, was traveling alone up the rutted and rugged highway from Alberta to the Yukon. Linda didn't know you don't travel to Whitehorse alone in a rundown Honda Civic, so she set off where only four-wheel-drives normally venture. The first evening she found a room in the mountains near a summit and asked for a 5 A.M. wakeup call so she could get an early start. She couldn't understand why the clerk looked surprised at that request, but as she awoke to early-morning fog shrouding the mountain tops, she understood.

Not wanting to look foolish, she got up and went to breakfast. Two truckers invited Linda to join them, and since the place was so small, she felt obliged. "Where are you headed?" one of the truckers asked.

"Whitehorse."

"In that little Civic? No way! This pass is *dangerous* in weather like this."

"Well, I'm determined to try," was Linda's gutsy, if not very informed, response.

"Then I guess we're just going to have to hug you," the trucker suggested.

Linda drew back. "There's no way I'm going to let you touch me!"

"Not like that!" The truckers chuckled. "We'll put one truck in front of you and one in the rear. In that way, we'll get you through the mountains." All that foggy morning Linda followed the two red dots in front of her and had the reassurance of a big escort behind as they made their way safely through the mountains.

Caught in the fog in our dangerous passage through life, we need to be "hugged." With fellow Christians who know the way and can lead safely ahead of us, and with others behind, gently encouraging us along, we, too, can pass safely.[22]

[21] Craig B. Larson, Editor. *Illustrations for Preaching & Teaching*, p.129.
[22] Ibid., p.87.

PRACTICAL ILLUSTRATIONS

10-147

ENCOURAGEMENT

Philemon 22-25

(*POSB: Introduction*)

Key People in Your Path

When is the last time you reminisced through an old school yearbook? As you studied each page, each picture, and drew on long forgotten memories, did you yearn to see those people again? Special friends move in different circles, move away, and even pass away. Will you ever see them again?

Over the course of time, God places key people in your path who add tremendous joy and significance to your life. But sometimes even they move on and all that remains are precious memories. Do not let the memories fade. Refresh them by looking back and reflecting on the special people whom God has brought your way.

10-148

ENCOURAGEMENT

Titus 1:1-4

(*POSB: Note 2, point 2*)

Motivating Others to Believe

Many a game has been lost, not during the game, but during the times of practice. The teams that practice hard and pay attention to their coach will stand a good chance of winning the game. Everyone who has played a team sport in school can probably relate to this locker room challenge given during a break in the action.

> "Come on team! You know the plays by heart. We've been practicing for this big game for years. Now is not the time to quit. The thing that's keeping us out of the game is a lack of concentration. We've got to quit fumbling the ball!"
> The coach was really getting intense. He knew in his heart he had the best team on the field, but they were not performing well at all. He could see it coming all week long. His players had taken a nonchalant attitude about practicing. They felt all they had to do was show up on game day and the victory would be theirs for the taking. Instead, they were caught off-guard and were being soundly beaten.

What would happen if your pastor had the chance to give a pep-talk during half-time? It might sound a little bit like this...

> "You believers are in something far more important than a simple game. You are fighting to win in an arena where the opponent is strong. In order to win, you must stick together as a team and not fumble away your life. You can't trust the world to encourage you, not to embrace the truth—because the world will not. Everyone of us has to encourage and challenge one another. Years ago, a football team was told to 'win one for the Gipper.' You can go even further and pledge to win one for the Lord Jesus."

Practical Illustrations

10-149

ENCOURAGEMENT

Titus 3:8-11

(POSB: Note 1)

Stirring Others To Good Works

Every church needs believers who stir others to do good works. So many good programs run out of energy when the newness wears off. The key to survival is not just getting the job done, but training others to take over when the leader is gone.

> Jane did not let the grass grow under her feet. Whenever she heard about a legitimate need within her department at work, or some occasion to be celebrated, she took it upon herself to do something about it. Whether it meant pitching in and helping someone at work, cooking a meal, organizing a baby shower, taking someone to the doctor, or just lending her shoulder to cry on, Jane was there. But Jane went a step further. Although she knew people at work counted on her to take charge of these situations, Jane always involved other people. She never did a good deed that she did not invite someone else to join her or help her. Why? Was Jane incapable of doing these projects, no matter how big or small, by herself? Not at all. Jane was perfectly capable. And sometimes it might have been easier to do it by herself. But Jane knew that she would not always be there. One day she might be out sick and there would be a need. Or one day she might relocate to another city, and so on. Jane knew it was just as important for her to involve and train others in her ministry of helping as it was for her to be faithful. It has been said that the first job anyone should do in any profession is to begin training his or her replacement. Whether the individual leaves because of promotion, sickness, transfer, or death, if he or she has left the position with no one to take over, he/she has failed.

Good programs and good people do not have to die out. If you seek God's will for your life, He will reveal what good works He wants you to do. Then it is up to you to do the good work and make others a part of your ministry. Your encouragement will stir other believers to do good works also.

10-150

END TIMES

2 Thessalonians 2:4-9

(POSB: Note 2)

No One Is Unsinkable

When the "unsinkable" Titanic hit an iceberg in the early 1900's, there was great loss of life. Before the accident, there was an arrogant sense of security in the integrity of the ship. There was little time for evacuation instructions and drills. More time was spent on having good fun and arranging the deck chairs than preparing for an emergency.

When the ship began to sink, panic filled the hearts of the passengers. Compounding the tragedy, there were not enough lifeboats for everyone. Consequently, hundreds drowned in the freezing waters of the North Atlantic.

PRACTICAL ILLUSTRATIONS

There are many who are sailing in dangerous waters today. But proper planning will spare many from God's judgment on the earth. As this world continues to sink into the abyss, the church is charged to reach the people of the earth for Christ. Failure to do so seals our destiny as a spiritual Titanic.

10-151

ENDURANCE

2 Timothy 1:6-12

(*POSB: Introduction*)

Responding to Hardship

Think for a moment. What is the hardest thing you have ever had to do? Did you have to be the bearer of bad news? Did you have to discipline someone when it would have been easier to just ignore the situation? Have you ever had to take a stand for what was right, even at great personal cost to you? When life gets hard, how do you respond? Many shrink away from hardship.

After a horrific winter blizzard, a long-time employee of a downtown bank managed to fight her way through the snow-bound streets to get to work. Throughout the day, her supervisor noticed her just sitting at her desk, doing nothing. Puzzled, the supervisor asked, "Why aren't you working?" Offended, the employee responded, "Do you expect me to work? Just getting here should count for something!"

There are many Christian believers who have the same attitude as this employee. After struggling to reach a certain level of growth and service, continuing to grow and serve is the last thing on their minds. Hardship and hard work are to be avoided at all costs. How about you? Are you willing to press on for the cause of the gospel—regardless of the cost?

10-152

ENDURANCE

2 Thessalonians 1:1-5

(*POSB: Note 6*)

Trials Produce Stamina

Have you ever thought to yourself, "I wish I could be stronger in my faith. I wish I could be a better Christian and really make a difference in people's lives"?

A certain man related this thought to God one day while praying.

You see, until that time he had been blessed in every area of life. It seemed everything he put his hand to was a success. He expressed a burden to reach out to people who had problems. He was frustrated that no one ever sought him out for counsel. As he meditated on this desire, the Lord spoke to him in that still, small voice that often comes to believers when praying. "No one seeks your counsel because they can't relate to someone who has no problems." On the surface, he had no major problems. He had a good job, a good education, and a loving family that was together.

"That's it!" he exclaimed. "I've gone about this all wrong. Lord, whatever it takes, help me to better relate to people." It was only a few days later that he unexpectedly lost his job.

PRACTICAL ILLUSTRATIONS

In another two months, his parents separated. On the way to run an errand, he was in a car accident. Little did he realize that God was answering his prayer by allowing these trials to touch his life—trials that others could relate to. Needless to say, the man was crushed, devastated by so much happening all at once. But God strengthened the man, carrying him through all the difficulties, working all things out for good.

From that simple desire to be used by God, he was sharpened and strengthened. In the following years, he was able to use the testimony of God's strength to encourage hundreds of people.

Are you willing to take a risk to prove yourself worthy?

❧

10-153

ETERNAL LIFE

2 Thessalonians 2:13-17   **Being on the Right Path**

(POSB: Introduction)

Have you ever had to wait in line in traffic, at the bank, or at the grocery store? Which line do you get into? The personal challenge is to make the best guess on which line will move the quickest.

If you guess wrongly, you might get impatient and disgruntled. But if you picked the quickest line, a feeling of great relief and satisfaction fills your mind—as you look at all the people who are still waiting.

Fortunately, when it comes to life, there is no guesswork about which line to choose. God picked the right line for you to stand in—the redemptive line of salvation, the line of eternal life that is rooted in His Son, the Lord Jesus Christ.

❧

10-154

ETERNITY

2 Timothy 2:8-13   **Your Choice: Life or Death?**

(POSB: Note 4)

God means what He says and His Word is true. Some people will respond to the invitation of Christ and say yes; sadly, others will respond and reject His invitation. This situation is graphically described in the following story.

During the blitz in London a woman stood in an open window in the top story of a blazing building. An escape ladder was quickly run up. A brave fireman made his way to the top. He leaned into the window with outstretched arms to take the woman to safety. The more he pleaded with her, the more she retreated in terror. The flames enveloped her. The noble fireman had to return without her! Weeping, he said, "I tried to save her, but she wouldn't let me!"[23]

Everyone will make an eternal choice. Will you choose eternal life or eternal condemnation?

❧

---

[23] *Sunday School Times.* Walter B. Knight. *Knight's Treasury of 2,000 Illustrations.* (Grand Rapids, MI: Eerdmans Publishing Company, 1992), p.210.

PRACTICAL ILLUSTRATIONS

10-155

1 Thessalonians 2:1-12   **Avoid Being a Spiritual Quack**

(POSB: Introduction)

When you are sick and have to go to the doctor, there is only one piece of paper in his office that really matters: his or her degree. Your confidence is not in the selection of magazines and brochures lying around on tables but this piece of paper that authenticates the doctor's ability to give you the care you need.

Your doctor did not just wake up one day and become a doctor. He or she had to go through years of school and training at great personal sacrifice. All of this was done with people just like you in mind. Your doctor would be of no help to you without that piece of paper. On the other hand, those who practice medicine without a license or a degree are known as "quacks" and will do more harm than good. Unwilling to pay the price, they settle for shortcuts at the expense of their patients.

Avoid being a spiritual quack. In a world sick with sin, there is a great shortage of qualified spiritual doctors. As believers we are to study the Word and to mature as Christians—boldly serving the people and declaring the gospel.

❧

10-156

EVANGELISM

1 Thessalonians 2:13-20   **Equipped to Be a Soul-winner**

(POSB: Note 5)

One night a man was driving his car when suddenly the headlights went out. Knowing that he was close to a service station, he turned on his emergency flashers and limped to the service station. After the mechanic made a quick inspection, he simply went to the fuse box and replaced a bad fuse with a good one. After paying his bill, the man drove home with plenty of light to show the way.

Many of us as believers are driving in darkness, failing to light the way for the lost, failing to be soul-winners. God has given us the right equipment, but somewhere along the way we have failed to plug in to the Source of light: the Lord Jesus Christ. Being a soul-winner is simply lighting the way...

- for a person to know Jesus Christ personally.
- for a person to conquer the sin and shame of this life.
- for a person to conquer the trials, tribulations, and temptations in this life.
- for a person to pass from death to life, to live eternally with God.
- for a person to get out of darkness and into the light.
- for a person to live a life of righteousness.

Would you consider yourself to be a soul-winner? Do not be intimidated by the term. Take comfort in the fact that God has promised to equip His people for His work.

❧

PRACTICAL ILLUSTRATIONS

10-157

EVANGELISM

1 Thessalonians 2:1-12

Willing to Suffer for the Gospel

(POSB: Note 2)

Are you bold in your witness, or do you tend to water down the message of the gospel so as to not offend anyone? Listen to this powerful testimony from one of the early church fathers:

> When the great Chrysostom was arrested by the Roman Emperor, the latter sought to make the Greek Christian recant, but without success. So the emperor discussed with his advisers what could be done to the prisoner. "Shall I put him in a dungeon?" the Emperor asked.
>
> "No," one of his counselors replied, "for he will be glad to go. He longs for the quietness wherein he can delight in the mercies of his God."
>
> "Then he shall be executed!" said the Emperor.
>
> "No," was the answer, "for he will also be glad to die. He declares that in the event of death he will be in the presence of his Lord."
>
> "What shall we do then?" the ruler asked.
>
> "There is only one thing that will give Chrysostom pain," the counselor said. "To cause Chrysostom to suffer, make him sin. He is afraid of nothing except sin."[24]

If you were in the same situation, what would the opposition say about your life, your witness? Would you, too, be bold in spreading the gospel? What gives *you* the greatest fear in your Christian witness?

10-158

FAITH

2 Timothy 1:6-12

Are You Walking the Walk?

(POSB: Note 5, point 3)

In the final analysis, our faith is relevant only if we are willing to put our lives on the line. Are you willing?

> This piece was heard on National Public Radio's *Morning Edition* on November 2, 1988:
>
> In 1958, America's first commercial jet air service began with the flight of the Boeing 707. A month after that first flight, a traveler on a...propeller-driven DC-6 airliner struck up a conversation with a fellow passenger.

---

[24] *Baptist Standard.* Paul Lee Tan. *Encyclopedia of 7,700 Illustrations: Signs of the Times*, p.282.

PRACTICAL ILLUSTRATIONS

The passenger happened to be a Boeing engineer. The traveler asked the engineer about the new jet aircraft, whereupon the engineer began speaking at length about the extensive testing Boeing had done on the jet engine before bringing it into commercial service. He recounted Boeing's experience with engines, from the B-17 to the B-52.

When his traveling companion asked him if he himself had yet flown on the new 707 jet airliner, the engineer replied, "I think I'll wait until it's been in service awhile."

Even enthusiastic talking about our faith doesn't mean much if we aren't also willing to put our lives where our mouth is.[25]

Are you truly walking the Christian walk or just talking the Christian talk?

10-159

FAITH

1 Thessalonians 3:1-10

(POSB: Note 4, point 4)

Faith That Inspires

Does your faith ever stir other believers? Listen to this story from the life of Hudson Taylor, a great missionary to inland China:

When Hudson Taylor...first went to China, it was in a sailing vessel. Very close to the shore of cannibal islands the ship was [calmed], and it was slowly drifting shoreward unable to go about, and the savages were eagerly anticipating a feast.

The captain came to Mr. Taylor and besought him to pray for the help of God. "I will," said Taylor, "provided you set your sails to catch the breeze." The captain declined to make himself a laughing stock by unfurling in a dead calm. Taylor said, "I will not undertake to pray for the vessel unless you will prepare the sails." And it was done.

While engaged in prayer, there was a knock at the door of his stateroom. "Who is there?" The captain's voice responded, "Are you still praying for wind?" "Yes." "Well," said the captain, "you'd better stop praying, for we have more wind than we can manage."[26]

Faith that stirs others is demonstrated by deliberate acts of reliance on God. A strong, stirring faith trusts God for every need.

---

[25] Craig B. Larson, Editor. *Illustrations for Preaching & Teaching*, p.79.

[26] *Oriental and Inter-American Missionary Standard.* Paul Lee Tan. *Encyclopedia of 7,700 Illustrations: Signs of the Times,* p.403-404.

PRACTICAL ILLUSTRATIONS

10-160

FAITH

1 Thessalonians 3:1-10

(POSB: Note 2, point 3)

Misplaced Faith Is Deadly

On what or whom is your faith focused? Making a wrong choice can prove to be fatal.

> In April 1988 the evening news reported on a photographer who was a skydiver. He had jumped from a plane along with numerous other skydivers and filmed the group as they fell and opened their parachutes. On the film shown on the telecast, as the final skydiver opened his chute, the picture went berserk. The announcer reported that the cameraman had fallen to his death, having jumped out of the plane without his parachute. It wasn't until he reached for the absent ripcord that he realized he was free-falling without a parachute.
>
> Until that point, the jump probably seemed exciting and fun. But tragically, he had acted with thoughtless haste and deadly foolishness. Nothing could save him, for his faith was in a parachute [that was] never buckled on. Faith in anything but an all-sufficient God can be just as tragic spiritually. Only with faith in Jesus Christ dare we step into the dangerous excitement of life.[27]

It is a tragic mistake to neglect Christ all through life's journey, then assume He will save you in the end. Be smart: place your faith in the Savior every day, then be ready to call on Him at a moment's notice.

☙

10-161

FAITH

2 Timothy 2:1-7

(POSB: Introduction)

Spiritual Fitness

Do you look good when you exercise? A marketing survey on the use of exercise clothing stated that less than 10% of the people bought the clothes for the sole purpose of exercising. This same survey noted that 35% bought exercise clothes for comfort and appearance only. Over half of those surveyed combined the use of the clothing for casual wear and exercise.

In reality, a jogging suit is more comfortable than a lot of the clothes we wear. But just wearing a comfortable and attractive exercise outfit will not make you stronger. Physical fitness comes to those who actually exercise.

This principle is also true for the spiritual fitness of the Christian believer. Outside appearances will not make you spiritually strong. You must exercise faith internally to be strong in the Lord.

☙

---

[27] Craig B. Larson, Editor. *Illustrations for Preaching & Teaching*, p.77.

PRACTICAL ILLUSTRATIONS

10-162

FAITH

1 Thessalonians 3:1-10

(POSB: Introduction)

The Testimony of a Strong Faith

Strong faith not only endures through difficult times, it becomes even stronger, knowing that God will care for every need.

The great preacher Charles Spurgeon was thinking over his great responsibilities one day, which caused him in a short time to be filed with worry and discouragement. Suddenly, however, as he meditated on the Scripture, "My grace is sufficient for thee," he began to laugh, realizing how silly it was to worry.

He began to illustrate in his mind, understanding that God's grace could not fail him any more than a fish in a river could run out of water, any more than a mouse in a grain silo could run out of food, or any more than a man on top of a mountain could run short of air. Spurgeon laughed and was greatly strengthened in his faith, because he realized that believers can enjoy the provision of heaven right here on earth.[28]

10-163

FAITHFULNESS

2 Thessalonians 3:1-5

(POSB: Note 2)

Evidence of God's Faithfulness

Most of us have lived long enough to be disappointed with people from time to time. But the Lord remains faithful. Even when you cannot clearly see Him, the Christian believer knows that God is ever so near and close by!

Picture a little girl flying a kite on the beach. She has her kite so high in the air that it looks like a speck in the white, cotton clouds.

Someone happens by and asks, "What are you doing?" "I'm flying a kite," the little girl answers. "I don't see anything. How do you know it's still there?" "Because, silly," the girl replies, "I can feel the kite tugging on my hand."

Similarly, when we have faith in God, we feel the tug of His presence even though we cannot see Him.

---

[28] Ruth Peters, Compiler. *Bible Illustrations: Illustrations of Bible Truths.* (Chattanooga, TN: AMG Publishers, 1998), #246.

PRACTICAL ILLUSTRATIONS

10-164

FAITHFULNESS

2 Timothy 4:9-22

(POSB: Note 1, point 1.g)

Standing with Fellow Believers

Caring about fellow believers means standing with them even in times of trial and pain, hurting when they hurt, feeling what they feel.

> A man passing a small group of children noticed they were all crying noisily. He stopped one lad and asked, "What's the trouble? Why are you all crying?" Between sobs the boy answered, "We all have a pain in Billy's stomach." That's real sympathy for the one who is suffering.[29]

∽

10-165

FAITHFULNESS

2 Thessalonians 3:1-5

(POSB: Introduction)

You Can Rely on God

Picture yourself serving the Lord on a foreign mission field. You find yourself constantly in trouble with the rulers of the country. All around you are fanatics whose lifestyle is hypocritical, repulsive, and downright pagan. You need help and you need it soon!

You have been given the chance to make one phone call to some close friends. Your time on the phone is limited to sixty seconds. What would you request from your friends? An immediate rescue? A transfer to another location? Personal relief in the way of supplies or a substitute? These are not bad suggestions, but the Apostle Paul did not choose any of them. Writing from the carnal city of Corinth, his burden focused on two items: prayer for successful ministry in Corinth and a helpful reminder that the Lord was faithful and in control.

Do your circumstances and surroundings ever get you down? Of course, we all experience times of disappointment and worry. But when you pray, pray for the advancement of the kingdom. And always keep in mind that God is securely on His throne. You can rely on the Lord in every situation.

∽

10-166

FALSE TEACHERS

Titus 1:10-16

(POSB: Introduction)

The Danger of False Teachers

"The Ten Most Wanted Men in America" are listed on posters in prominent public buildings (like the U.S. Post Office for example). Photographs of these criminals are shown in order to alert law-abiding citizens of their danger and to arouse the help of the public in locating these criminals.

---

[29] Ruth Peters, Compiler. *Bible Illustrations: Book One—Illustrations of Bible Truths.* (Chattanooga, TN: AMG Publishers, 1995), #427.

PRACTICAL ILLUSTRATIONS

Now think for a moment: Would you want to invite one of these dangerous criminals into your home? Of course not. It would be a very foolish thing to do. If you did happen to see one of these criminals, it would be your civic duty to report the information to the police.

A false teacher is just as dangerous to the church as a criminal is to the community. But unfortunately the zeal that is displayed when a person reports criminals to the police is rarely seen when it comes to dealing with false teachers in God's house.

In order to protect the church, God has posted a "Most Wanted" list in His Word. Therefore, the Christian believer has strict instructions to be on the lookout for these spiritual criminals.

10-167

FALSE TEACHERS

1 Timothy 4:1-5

(POSB: Introduction)

How to Detect a Counterfeit

What can be done to protect Christian believers from the evil tentacles of false teachers? The answer is simpler than you might think: spend a lot of time handling the truth. Dr. Walter Martin gives this illustration:

> The American Banking Association has a training program....Each year it sends hundreds of bank tellers to Washington in order to teach them to detect counterfeit money, which is a great source of a loss of revenue to the Treasury Department. "It is most interesting that during the entire two-week training program, no teller touches counterfeit money. Only the original passes through his hands. The reason for this is that the American Banking Association is convinced that if a man is thoroughly familiar with the original, he will not be deceived by the counterfeit bill, no matter how much like the original it appears."[30]

10-168

FALSE TEACHERS

1 Timothy 4:1-5

(POSB: Note 2, point 3)

An Instrument of God or of the Devil?

William Barclay has an excellent statement on men becoming tools of Satan and evil spirits.

> It was from these evil spirits and demons that...false teaching came. But though it came from the demons, it came through men.... Now here is the threatening and the terrible thing. We know that God and God's Spirit are everywhere looking for men to use. God is always searching for men who will be His instruments, His weapons, His tools in the world. But here we come face to face with the terrible fact that the forces of evil are also looking for men to use. Just as God seeks men for His purposes, the

[30] Walter R. Martin. *The Kingdom of the Cults.* (Minneapolis, MN: Bethany House Publishers, 1982), p.16.

forces of evil seek men for their purposes. Here is the terrible responsibility of manhood. Man can accept the service of God, or the service of the devil. Man can become an instrument of the Supreme Good or the Supreme Evil. Men are faced with the eternal choice—to whom are we to give our lives, to God or to God's enemy? Are we to decide to be used by God, or are we to decide to be used by the devil? [31]

10-169

FALSE TEACHERS

1 Timothy 1:3-11   **The Source of Truth**

(POSB: Note 4)

We must never forget that the Bible is our only reliable guide for truth. No person can be the authority on truth, no matter how much education or experience he has. As A.W. Tozer said:

> The devil is a better theologian than any of us and is a devil still.[32]

10-170

FALSE TEACHERS

1 Timothy 1:3-11   **Worse than Benedict Arnold**

(POSB: Introduction)

There are few things that can turn the stomach of a nation more than that of a traitor. Remember Benedict Arnold? Arnold, as you may recall, was an American who spied on his own countrymen during the Revolutionary War. He was found guilty of treason and executed.

But note: as bad as Arnold's betrayal was, a false teacher who operates in the church is even more repulsive. While Arnold's betrayal of America was a temporary thing, a false teacher's damage to the Kingdom of God is eternal because he leads souls away from God into everlasting damnation.

---

31 William Barclay. *The Letters to Timothy, Titus, and Philemon*, p.107.

32 A.W. Tozer. *Man: The Dwelling Place of God.* (Carol Stream, Il: Christianity Today), Vol. 41, No.5.

PRACTICAL ILLUSTRATIONS

10-171

FAMILY

2 Timothy 1:1-5

(POSB: Note 6)

A Good Heritage

Parents have a serious charge from God to implant scriptural teaching in their children. Listen to the sound godly advice behind the words of Bill Hybels:

> "We're here," the man said warmly to his wife. "Copacabana Beach, the top floor, a beautiful restaurant and a first-class hotel. It's been worth it, hasn't it honey? Working and saving all these years were worth it for a night like tonight."
>
> I couldn't help overhearing this couple at the table next to mine as I sat alone, thinking about all I'd seen over the previous few weeks. I was on the last leg of a month-long trip my father had sent me on throughout Central and South America to deliver money to missionaries he was supporting there. And since I was going that direction, he'd put together an itinerary with stops in several cities throughout South America just so I could more fully experience that part of the world.
>
> It was a very formative time in my life. I was nineteen years old. I'd recently become a Christian but didn't know yet what I was going to do for the rest of my life. I'd begun the journey with a tribe of Indians in the middle of the Central American jungle where a church was flourishing. It was an exciting place. The Holy Spirit was active, and lives were being changed throughout the whole region.
>
> ...I felt almost dizzy as I thought to myself, "Wait a minute. These people are about sixty years old, and they're saying they've waited a lifetime to experience *this?* I'm nineteen and I'm already sitting here! What am I going to do for the next thirty or forty years? If this is *It,* I'm in big trouble. It's nice, but it certainly isn't *It.*
>
> I remember walking back to my room thinking, "What am I going to do with my life? What's important enough for me to invest my whole future in?
>
> ...By comparison I thought back to that little church in the middle of the jungle, and the number of really sharp people who had given their lives to serve among those Indians....I remembered sitting on the ground just days earlier during one of their worship services as they sang their hearts out in praise to God.
>
> That night...I realized that what I'd seen happening in that tribe was more real, more lasting, and more important than just rolling up the score in the business world. And it was something I wanted to be a part of.
>
> As it turned out, that was a thought I was never able to shake, in spite of all the allurements and opportunities that would pull me in other directions.[33]

Nothing can take the place of being thoroughly grounded in the principles of God's Word. It is the best possible inheritance a parent can give.

---

33 Bill Hybels and Mark Mittelberg. *Becoming a Contagious Christian.* (Grand Rapids, MI: Zondervan Publishing House, 1994), pp.211-212.

PRACTICAL ILLUSTRATIONS

10-172

FEAR

2 Timothy 1:6-12   ## Overcoming Fear

(POSB: Note 2)

Many believers allow fear to curb their relationship with the Lord. Fear acts as a barrier, an obstacle to total trust in Christ. Listen closely to this story that contrasts fear with faith.

Needy miners and settlers in British Columbia, engaged in stripping an abandoned fort...of lumber, electrical appliances, and plumbing, made an amazing discovery. While dismantling the jail they found that...mighty locks were attached to the heavy doors, and two-inch steel bars covered the windows, but the walls of the prison were only...wallboard of clay and paper, painted to resemble iron. A good old heave against the walls by a man not as strong as a football tackle would have burst the wall out. Nobody ever tried it because nobody thought it possible.

Many Christians are prisoners of fears that are nothing when pushed against. Satan cannot do anything against a child of God, but he loves to put barriers of papier-mâché in the path of the believer to make him think that there is no progress in the direction of the will of the Lord. When by faith we push against it we will be free.[34]

If fear has you locked up, faith in God will set you free.

༺ঌ

10-173

FELLOWSHIP

1 Thessalonians 2:13-20   ## The Drawing Power of Love

(POSB: Note 4)

How much does meeting with other believers mean to you? Do you have a vibrant passion to meet with God's people, or do you take your fellowship for granted?

There is a story about a man who walked miles to get to his church. Waymon was the kind of guy who had a hard time fitting into the "right" social circles. The truth be known, you might even have had a hard time accepting him into your group if you were the type of person who judged a book by its cover.

Fortunately, Waymon's church was flexible enough to look beyond his rough edges and accept him as a part of the flock. The church that Waymon chose to be his family was considered to be a pretty affluent group. But their affluence did not blind them with pride.

Waymon was a whole lot more reliable than many members. The weather did not keep him away. He was always there to help set up the chairs and do anything that would make the worship service a meaningful experience.

---

[34] *Eternity.* Walter B. Knight. *Knight's Master Book of 4,000 Illustrations.* (Grand Rapids, MI: Eerdmans Publishing Company, 1994), p. 217.

PRACTICAL ILLUSTRATIONS

Why did Waymon love to come to church? He loved to come to church because in that place he found the love and acceptance which was not his out in the world.

Would you walk a mile or more for love?

❧

10-174

FINANCIAL SUPPORT

1 Timothy 5:17-20

(POSB: Introduction)

Mistreating God's Servants

How do you feel when you hear about an animal being abused? Anyone with a tender heart is sickened when a pet has been mistreated. Animal abuse occurs daily: everything from kicking a cat to starving a dog. Would any true animal lover do these kinds of things? Of course not.

On the other hand, what emotions fill your heart when you hear about one of God's servants being mistreated—whether through neglect or a direct attack? Would a person who professes to follow Christ ever criticize one of God's servants? Is it possible that a church would do this? Unfortunately, it happens far too often.

This is a day in which the minister of God is being attacked, attacked not only by the world but, most unfortunately, by those within the church. The attackers are causing a loss of respect for Christ and a persecution of the ministry that has seldom been experienced in civilization. Because of this, ministers are being neglected when it comes to meeting their financial needs and quickly deserted when gossip and rumors swirl about. Whether the rumors are true or not is often not even considered. Prayer and financial support for the minister of God are simply dropped. This is the work of the devil. The Christian believer must not take part in such diabolical abuse.

❧

10-175

FINANCIAL SUPPORT

1 Timothy 5:17-20

(POSB: Note 1)

Support Your Local Pastor

There is probably no more awkward time for the minister than when he has to negotiate his salary. Some churches live by the adage, "Keep 'em humble. Keep 'em poor." Here is one story to illustrate this point.

A pastor's search committee was interviewing one particular candidate for their church. They were impressed by what the man brought to the table as a minister. He could preach, teach, and fulfill all the other pastoral duties in a professional manner.

As the interview came to a close, the chairman of the committee tossed out one final question, "Approximately how much money will it take for you to make it financially?" The minister gave him a very reasonable figure that his denomination had suggested to him. The committee chairman took a deep breath and said, "That's a little bit more than we had in mind. We feel that a preacher can live off what we offer and then let faith do the rest."

At first, the minister did not say a word. But under his breath he prayed for wisdom. When he felt confident that God had given him a word to share, he looked each person in the eye and said, "Would *you* be willing to work for what you just offered me and let faith do the rest?"

Is your church being fair financially to your pastor, or is it trying to pay him as little as possible?

❧

10-176

FOOLISHNESS

Titus 3:3   **Fool or Follower?**

(POSB: Note 1)

What conclusion would you draw about someone who took late-night walks down dangerous alleys—all alone? You would rightly conclude that the person was foolish. Likewise, whenever anyone attempts to walk in this world without God, he is just as foolish.

The story is told of a rich young man who prided himself in being current on the latest trends and fads. One such trend was to follow a certain man with radical ideas. He challenged his followers to live life free from the lusts of the world.

The young man made it a personal priority to meet the leader to inquire about joining. After answering a few questions, the leader said, "Fine. We'd love to have you join us. We will expect your membership dues at once."

"Membership dues? Sure. How much should I write my check for?" the rich young man asked. The answer shocked him. "If you want to join our group, go and sell all that you have and give the proceeds to the poor." "You're kidding, aren't you?" the young man wished aloud. His face dropped and he walked away. Some who were there that day overheard him say, "I don't need to join his group. I can make it on my own."

Every community and every generation has its share of rich young rulers who choose to go it alone without Christ. And every one of them, without exception, is a fool. Only God can turn a fool into a follower. Which one are you?

❧

10-177

FORGIVENESS

1 Timothy 1:12-17   **Being an Ambassador of Christ**

(POSB: Note 1, point 2)

William Barclay has an excellent message for us as believers as we deal with dear brothers and sisters who have fallen.

It was to Paul an amazing thing, that he, the arch-persecutor, had been chosen as the missionary and the pioneer of Christ. It was not only that Jesus Christ had forgiven

PRACTICAL ILLUSTRATIONS

him; it was that Christ had trusted him. Sometimes in human affairs we forgive a man who has committed some mistake or who has been guilty of some sin, but we make it very clear that his past makes it impossible for us to trust him again with any responsibility. But Christ had not only forgiven Paul, He had entrusted him with His work to do. The man who had been the persecutor of Christ had been made the ambassador of Christ.[35]

We must be as faithful and forgiving to others as Christ is to us!

10-178

FOUNDATION

2 Thessalonians 1:1-5

(POSB: Note 2)

Build on a Firm Foundation

Jesus has warned believers: if they build their lives on sand, the storms of life will wash them away (Matthew 7:26-27). This vivid point has been illustrated time and again by those who have built expensive homes on the beach.

Years ago, a man ignored the advice of his financial counselor and his building contractor. He invested a good part of his life's savings in building a magnificent home with a great view of the ocean. For him, the closer to the ocean the better. In fact, he built his home right on the beach.

When storm season arrived, a devastating hurricane hit and totally destroyed his home. As he surveyed his loss, a reporter asked him: "Why did you take the risk of building your home so close to the water?" With a heavy heart he replied, "I just never thought a storm would hit this beach in my lifetime."

Contrary to some popular beliefs, Christians are not exempt from the storms of life. We have no choice about some of the storms that come our way, but we do have a choice about *where* we build our lives: on the solid Rock of Jesus Christ or upon the shifting sands of this world.

10-179

FRIENDSHIP

2 Timothy 1:13-18

(POSB: Note 4)

Be a Faithful Friend

Who is your most *faithful* friend? Listen to this stirring example about the pursuit of friendship.

A traveling salesman came to a small community to sell his products. As his rickety truck came to a stop, a crowd of customers surrounded him.

---

[35] William Barclay. *The Letters to Timothy, Titus, and Philemon.* (Philadelphia, PA: The Westminster Press, 1960), p.48.

As the people pressed in to examine the goods, he advertised his newest item. "Hurry, hurry, hurry," he cried out. "Step right up and see for yourself this *Faithful Friendship Kit.* Come get 'em while they last."

Not surprisingly, he sold every one he had on his truck that day. As the people opened up their kits at home, they were quickly disappointed. The *Faithful Friendship Kits* were empty—except for a small piece of paper that read:
- If you want a faithful friend, you must first *become* one.
- If you become a faithful friend, it will get you a *new* one.
- You've got to put *yourself* into it: make a fresh commitment to love people and to use things, not to use people and to love things.

A few of the people were outraged and demanded their money back. Others just missed the point altogether and let the matter drop. But there were some who got the salesman's point and took the matter to heart.

How about you? Is there still something missing in your *Faithful Friendship Kit*? Could it be you?

❧

10-180

FRUITFULNESS

Titus 1:1-4

(POSB: Note 4)

The Desire to Produce Fruit

Only a foolish farmer would plant a crop that he knew would not grow or bear fruit. In the same line of thought, would a Christian be wise if he spent his time doing things that were unproductive, that bore no fruit and produced no disciples? Of course not! Unfortunately, the lack of fruit in the lives of many Christians is an indictment against them. But here is the story of one man who truly caught the vision of reproducing.

Dick was a fairly young Christian, but his immaturity did not prevent him from getting excited about serving Christ. In fact, he got very excited when an opportunity came for him to share his testimony. He loved to tell how God came into his life and saved him.

Dick was discipled by a man who believed in the Biblical principle of multiplication. His spiritual mentor met with him every week for three months, and encouraged him in the Christian life. Dick was convinced that his experience was too precious to keep to himself. So Dick took what he had learned and sought out two other believers to disciple them—and in turn taught them to reach out to disciple others. The most wonderful thing happened as a result: the chain of reaching and discipling others for Christ marched on and on and continues even today.

The fruit that the Bible talks about sometimes comes by the slow process of addition. But the real key to spiritual growth is found in multiplication. The challenge for the Christian believer is simple: your life is a testimony before others—either positive or negative, either good or bad. Is your testimony fruitful, drawing others to Christ and helping them grow? Or is your testimony fruitless, either misleading others or leading them nowhere?

❧

PRACTICAL ILLUSTRATIONS

10-181

GODLINESS

1 Timothy 4:6-16

(POSB: Note 4)

Breaking Free from Sin

As believers, we live in a constant spiritual tension. On one hand, we need to be good stewards of our bodies, of the temple that God has provided for us to live in. But on the other hand, as Martin Luther once said, the believer only *dwells* in the flesh but does not *live* in it. Therefore, we must pursue godliness and inner spiritual maturity.

> Eric was a professional football player whose body was like granite. From his youth, he was committed to exercise and to excellence on the field of competition. In the eyes of the world Eric had it made. But he wisely knew there was much more to life than scoring touchdowns.
>
> Eric's earlier encounter with Jesus Christ had challenged him to work just as hard getting his spiritual life in shape. He later felt a leading from the Lord to become a pastor, and as his spirit matured, so did his witness and boldness. The urban streets of his city became his personal parish. For example, he would often put on a display for the kids in a neighborhood. In a powerful demonstration of physical versus spiritual strength, he would break free from a set of handcuffs. Then he would explain how Jesus Christ gave him the power to break free from the sin that had held him in shackles.

What is the focus of exercise in your life? You must carefully balance the physical and spiritual to be sure that the fruit you bear is first of all godliness.

10-182

GODLINESS

1 Timothy 6:11-16

(POSB: Introduction)

Living a Godly Life

In the mid-1950's there was a popular American television program called "To Tell the Truth." Three guests on the show would claim to be the same person. Four panelists would then ask the guests questions to determine who was telling the truth. After a set time was up, each panelist voted for his or her choice as to who was telling the truth. Then the host of the show asked, "Will the real...[John Doe or whoever] please stand up?"

In many ways, this game is being played out in churches throughout the world. People are presenting themselves or claiming to be godly. Is there a sure way to know who is telling the truth? How can we know who is truly a godly person? If we know the right questions to ask, we will be able to pick the right person, the godly man or woman who will stand up and be counted as such. Where are those questions to be found? Right in God's Word. There is a straightforward charge to the Christian believer to be a "man of God." What a dynamic challenge!

PRACTICAL ILLUSTRATIONS

10-183

GODLINESS

1 Timothy 4:6-16   **What Makes a Good Minister?**

(POSB: Introduction)

Exactly what is it that makes a person a *good minister*? Is it the number of degrees that hang on his wall. Is it where he went to school? Does his denominational choice (or lack of a denomination) make him a good minister? Or the books and files in his library? How about his willingness to visit people in the church?

All of these are good things, but in and of themselves they do not have the power to make a minister good. A minister who wants to be good makes a quality decision at the foot of the cross and applies the commands of Scripture to his life. He takes seriously the charge of God to strive for godliness, and that godliness is what makes a minister good.

10-184

GOSPEL

1 Thessalonians 1:5-10   **Living Out the Gospel Practically**

(POSB: Note 1)

The Apostle Paul was committed to preach the gospel and to minister to the practical needs of people. Listen to this contemporary example as told by Ralph Neighbor:

> Jack had been president of a large corporation, and when he got cancer, [the company] ruthlessly dumped him. He went through his insurance, used his life savings, and had practically nothing left.
>
> I visited him with one of my deacons, who said, "Jack, you speak so openly about the brief life you have left. I wonder if you've prepared for your life after death?"
>
> Jack stood up, livid with rage. "You—Christians. All you ever think about is what's going to happen to me after I die. If your God is so great, why doesn't he do something about the real problems of life?" He went on to tell us he was leaving his wife penniless and his daughter without money for college. Then he ordered us out.
>
> Later my deacon insisted we go back. We did.
>
> "Jack, I know I offended you," he said. "I humbly apologize. But I want you to know I've been working since then. Your first problem is where your family will live after you die. A realtor in our church has agreed to sell your house and give your wife his commission.
>
> "I guarantee you that, if you'll permit us, some other men and I will make the house payments until it's sold.
>
> "Then, I've contacted the owner of an apartment house down the street. He's offered your wife a three-bedroom apartment plus free utilities and an $850-a-month salary in return for her collecting rents and supervising plumbing and electrical repairs. The income from your house should pay for your daughter's college. I just wanted you to know your family will be cared for."
>
> Jack cried like a baby.

He died shortly thereafter, so wrapped in pain he never accepted Christ. But he experienced God's love even while rejecting him. And his widow, touched by the caring Christians, responded to the gospel message.[36]

Paul lived out the gospel in his everyday life—through the power of the Holy Spirit. His lifestyle, carried out in boldness and assurance, was an example to believers and unbelievers alike. The challenge for every believer to ask himself is this: Do others see Jesus in me?

10-185

GRACE

2 Thessalonians 3:6-18

Escaping the Penalty of Sin

(POSB: Note 4)

The grace of God makes it possible for us to escape the penalty of sin. Author Patsy Clairmont reminds her readers that grace gives the believer another chance:

I was so familiar with our five-mile stretch of country road into town that I developed a rhythm to my driving. Sometimes my rhythm was faster than the posted pace. After following me into town on several occasions, Les [her husband] mentioned I needed to lighten up on my footwork.

At times when I drove to town, I wouldn't remember the ride in because I was on autopilot. I knew every curve and turn by heart, and my mind tended to wander.

Often I would sing my way to town, and if the song happened to be a bouncy one, without realizing it, I would drive to the beat. This wasn't a problem if I was singing "How Great Thou Art." However, when I got into the rousing chorus of "I'll Fly Away," my little wagon seemed to be doing that very thing. Les warned me more than once to pay closer attention to my selections.

On one particularly beautiful autumn day, I was on my way to speak for an area woman's retreat. My six-year-old, Jason, was in the back seat, looking forward to seeing his friends at the child-care room. I was into the rhythm of the road while I rehearsed my opening thoughts with great enthusiasm.

I glanced in my rearview mirror as something beckoned for my attention. There I spotted someone else who seemed to be quite enthusiastic in his desire to share some thoughts with me. A colorful character. I could tell by the red and blue circular lights on his car.

As he approached my car, I couldn't help chuckling as I pictured Les doing the "I told you so" nod.

Jason questioned, "Mom, why are you laughing?"

"Oh, honey, it's just Daddy told me that would happen one day."

The nice officer was not laughing. He leaned down and boomed with a voice that instantly reduced me to a teeny person, "And where are you going in such a hurry?"

---

[36] As told by Ralph Neighbor from the book *Death and the Caring Community*, by Larry Richards and Paul Johnson. Craig B. Larson, Editor. *Illustrations for Preaching & Teaching* , pp.68-69.

I meekly looked into his convicting face and whispered, "Church."

"You're kidding!" he bellowed.

"I'm the speaker," I confessed. "My topic is 'Renewed Living.' I guess I'm not doing too well...with it," I trailed off, wishing I could disappear.

He asked me a series of intelligent questions that I could not answer with any degree of accuracy—things like "Where is your car registration?" and "Where is your title?"

I was totally in the wrong, which was obvious to all of us.

So I was amazed when he announced, "I'm going to let you go without a ticket, but you must slow down and place the proper papers in your car."

That day the officer was Jesus. He extended mercy when I didn't deserve it.[37]

And that is the glory of grace—receiving what you don't deserve!

10-186

GRACE

2 Thessalonians 1:1-5

(POSB: Note 3)

God's Riches at Christ's Expense

Grace has been defined by some as: "God's Riches at Christ's Expense." It is impossible to understand grace unless we come to realize that it is by no means cheap. The grace of God is very expensive.

One day during the heat of military battle, a live grenade was thrown into the midst of a platoon. Stricken with fear, the men instinctively dove for cover. But in an instant, one of the soldiers made a choice to dive on top of the grenade. Absorbing the lethal fragments of death, his act of heroism saved the lives of the other men that day. His act of grace gave his friends an opportunity to live long and fruitful lives.

In the same sense, that is what God has done for us through Christ. He sent His Son into the war of the world for the souls of men, to absorb the lethal fragments of our sin. Upon the cross, He actually bore our sins for us. A grenade that would have killed mankind for eternity was neutralized by God's love for us. God actually gave His Son to die upon the cross for our sins. Because of Christ's sacrifice, we can have abundant life.

Christ gave His all that you might live. Are you enjoying the grace and peace that His death has made possible?

---

[37] Patsy Clairmont. *God Uses Cracked Pots.* (Pomona, CA: Focus on the Family Publishing, 1991), pp.61-62.

PRACTICAL ILLUSTRATIONS

10-187

GRACE

Titus 2:11-15

(POSB: Note 5)

Grace for the Prodigal

Scripture clearly instructs the believer to proclaim the grace of God. But grace cannot be accurately proclaimed if the proclaimer has never experienced God's grace. Listen carefully to this story.

The setting is a modern-day ranch. The wealthy father and his two sons, Pete and Ernie, were well-known in the county in which they lived.

Like a lot of wealthy boys, Pete and Ernie took their father's wealth for granted. They were young adults who longed for the day when Dad would set them up in their own business. With a good investment from Dad, they could enjoy the good life—without having to keep Dad's rules.

Pete was the bold brother. One day he decided to approach his father and state his case. "Dad, I'm ready to go it alone. I really need to spread my wings and fly. I know I'm in your will, but I don't want to wait until you die to get my start in business. I want it now."

Pete's father agreed to his son's request and gave him the money he demanded. Pete wasted no time enjoying his inheritance. He gave no thought to how he spent his money. Before long, Pete crashed in a heap of financial ruin. After he had wasted his last dime in a terrible investment, Pete decided to declare bankruptcy. He had nothing to show for the time and money he had spent. He thought about going home for awhile as a hired hand. As he thought about going home, he tried to anticipate his father's response: "See! I told you so. You wanted to do things your own way. You've made your bed—now sleep in it!" His brother Ernie was the pious one. Pete could just hear him say, "Pete, eat your heart out. You are broke and I'm rich. I might consider giving you a job at minimum wage."

Despite the response he imagined receiving, he decided to go back home and take his chances. As Pete walked down the long, straight drive to his father's ranch, he noticed a man running toward him. He soon recognized the man as his Dad.

Before Pete had a chance to figure what was going on, his father cried out, "Pete! Welcome home. I've really missed you." "Dad, did you hear what happened?" "Son, I know all about it. Anybody can make a mistake," said Pete's father in comforting tones. "Dad, I need a job. I'll take anything you've got."

The father laughed with joy. "I'll tell you what I've got for you. A job you'll be proud of and a beautiful new horse. I want you to have it. And you've got to be hungry. Let me tell the cook to prepare the biggest cow on the ranch. We're going to have a party!"

Pete was taken aback. "Dad, I don't understand. I don't deserve any of this. Why?" "Because I thought I had lost you forever. I've always loved you and I always will. Welcome home!" From that moment on, Pete became a much-sought-after speaker for those who were touched by his story of grace.

God had branded or touched the father's heart with grace, and now he was passing it on to his son. Have you been branded by God's grace? Unless you have, you will never be able to share it with others.

❧

PRACTICAL ILLUSTRATIONS

10-188

GRACE

Titus 2:11-15

(POSB: Introduction)

Help in the Time of Need

All of you have probably had at least one flat tire on your car. It is very deflating to your plans when you have to change the flat. These kinds of thoughts probably flood your mind: "I haven't got time for this....I'm going to be late....Why me, Lord?...How far can I drive on this thing?" But driving your car with a flat tire will cause further damage to your wheel. So you decide to spend the needed time to change your tire. However, when you open your trunk, you quickly realize that the spare tire is just as flat as the one on your car. You are unprepared, helpless, stranded. There you sit—unable to help yourself.

As other cars race by, you wonder how long you will have to sit until help comes. Finally, a police car pulls up behind you and the policeman offers his help. He is prepared for just such emergencies, and before long your tire is changed and you are on your way again.

At times, the Christian life can go through a similar setback. You can be rolling along fine in life and suddenly things go wrong; you find yourself unprepared and helpless. Does that mean you cannot recover? No, but when you cannot help yourself, you need the help of someone who *can* bring you through the trial or difficult situation victoriously. You need someone who can protect you from the fiery darts of Satan, who can carry you through the flood, who can lift you up out of the miry clay. You *need* the grace of God, the grace that brings salvation and direction and purpose to the life of the believer.

❧

10-189

GRACE

Titus 2:11-15

(POSB: Note 4)

How Deep Is God's Grace?

Is it even possible to grasp all God has done for you? The grace of God becomes even clearer when you realize how low Christ stooped to save you.

A farmer named Buck wanted to know how to get to heaven. He had heard different things from different people, but he wanted to know for sure. On one of his trips to town, Buck stopped by to see his friend Larry, the mechanic, whose Christian witness was known to almost everyone. "Larry, tell me what I need to do to get to heaven." Larry welcomed the opportunity to answer the farmer's question.

"Buck, if you fell into a deep, dark pit, broke your legs, and were unable to get out, what kind of help would you need?" "Well, I'd need somebody to come down and get me out." "Exactly" said Larry.

"But, if a person came by who went strictly by the law, he would yell down something like this: 'You have no business being in this pit. You should have kept your eyes open and watched where you were walking. You fell in by yourself, so figure how to get out by

63

yourself. Keep working and eventually you will make it. And if you ever get out, I hope you'll learn your lesson.' Then he would politely excuse himself and walk on.

"If someone came by who believed you have to work your way to heaven, he would yell down, 'If you can climb up half way, I'll help pull you up the rest of the way.'

"Buck, what good are either of these men to you?" "Why, none at all" said Buck. "They haven't done me a bit of good."

"Buck, I'll tell you exactly what you need. You need a man who will not condemn you for being in the pit. You need a man who will not force you to climb out by yourself. You need a man who will go down into the pit and lift you out. That man is Jesus Christ. Only Christ can save you. He has gone down into the pit of your sinful heart and pulled you out. He willingly paid the penalty for you sin and died on the cross in your place. That is the kind of help you need. That is the kind of Savior you need."

God's grace runs deep. No matter how dark the pit, no matter how deep the sin, Christ has demonstrated His grace by His sacrifice on the cross. His grace is at work even today for those who have fallen into the pit of sin. If you are in that pit, do not cry out for the legalist or for the one who makes you work your way out. Instead, cry out for the only One who can lift you out—the Lord Jesus Christ.

ೲ

10-190

GRACE

2 Timothy 2:1-7

(POSB: Note 1)

Looking for Unlimited Strength

A foreigner named Ezra came to America and was invited to tour sites exhibiting great power and strength. Ezra's host, Bob, first took him to see the nuclear power plant and said, "Ezra, within this nuclear power plant is enough power to provide electricity for the entire state." Ezra pulled out a notepad and scribbled a note.

Their next stop was a large military base. "Ezra, these soldiers and many more like them make us the strongest country on the face of the earth," Bob boasted as he showed Ezra around. As before, Ezra pulled out his notepad and scribbled another note.

Observing how impressed Ezra was, Bob then took him to the seat of political power and strength—the nation's capitol. "Ezra, the most powerful men in the world work here. Can't you just sense the strength of this city? It's almost intoxicating," Bob said. Once again Ezra took pen and paper and scribbled a note.

When it came time for Ezra to return to his own country, Bob was curious and said, "Tell me Ezra, were you impressed by the sources of power and strength I showed you? I noticed you took careful notes at each place we visited. If I may ask, what were your comments?"

Ezra pulled out his notepad and read these notes to Bob:

- Concerning the nuclear power plant—eventually, its strength will fail.
- Concerning the soldiers—eventually, they will die.
- Concerning the politicians—eventually, their power will corrupt them and they will fall or be voted out of power or retire and their power will be no more.

PRACTICAL ILLUSTRATIONS

"Bob, each of these sources of strength and power have limitations. If you are trusting in these, then *your* strength will be limited also."

What sources of strength and power impress you? Are you looking for strength in the things of this world or strength through the grace of God?

10-191

GRACE

2 Timothy 4:9-22

(POSB: Note 2, point 5)

The Provision of Salvation

"Grace be with you." What a great way to say farewell—to bless someone with the grace of God. It is a grace that refuses to let go! It is a grace not due to anything we have done on our own. Songwriter Bill Gaither paints this great picture of what the grace of God does for the Christian believer:

> Gloria and I had been married for a couple of years. We were teaching school in Alexandria, Indiana, where I had grown up, and we wanted a piece of land where we could build a house. I noticed the parcel south of town where cattle grazed, and I learned it belonged to a 92-year-old retired banker named Mr. Yule. He owned a lot of land in the area, and the word was he would sell none of it. He gave the same speech to everyone who inquired: "I promised the farmers they could use it for their cattle"....I introduced myself and told him we were interested in a piece of his land. "Not selling," he said pleasantly. "Promised it to a farmer for grazing...."
> He pursed his lips and stared at me. "What'd you say your name was?"
> "Gaither. Bill Gaither." "Hmmm. Any relation to Grover Gaither?" "Yes, sir. He was my granddad." Mr. Yule put down his paper and removed his glasses. "Interesting. Grover Gaither was the best worker I ever had on my farm. Full day's work for a full day's pay. So honest. What'd you say you wanted?"
> Nearly three decades later, my son and I strolled that beautiful, lush property that had once been pasture land. "Benjy," I said, "you've had this wonderful place to grow up through nothing that you've done, but because of the good name of a great-granddad you never met."[38]

In a similar way, the grace of God provides for the believer something we could never have attained on our own—eternal salvation in the good name of Jesus Christ our Lord.

---

[38] *Leadership Journal*, Summer 1993, Vol. 14, p. 61.

PRACTICAL ILLUSTRATIONS

10-192

HATE

Titus 3:3

(POSB: Note 4)

Only Christ Can Defuse Hate

A person who is hateful will, by definition, do hateful things. And a person who is *full* of hate, refusing to yield to Christ, is like a bomb waiting to explode. In a 1994 article, *Wars' Lethal Leftovers Threaten Europeans*, Associated Press reporter Christopher Burns wrote:

> The bombs of World War II are still killing in Europe. They turn up—and sometimes blow up—at construction sites, in fishing nets, or on beaches fifty years after the guns fell silent. "Hundreds of tons of explosives are recovered every year in France alone. Thirteen old bombs exploded in France last year, killing twelve people and wounding eleven," the Interior Ministry said.
>
> "I've lost two of my colleagues," said Yvon Bouvet, who heads a government team in the...region that defuses explosives from both World War I and II...."Unexploded bombs become more dangerous with time," Bouvet said. "With the corrosion inside, the weapon becomes more unstable, the detonator can be exposed."[39]

Hatred is a lit fuse that will unleash every sin in the human heart. There is only one person who can safely deactivate this deadly bomb called hate. It is Jesus Christ Himself. Christ threw His life on sin and took on the full impact of its lethal effects.

10-193

HOLINESS

1 Timothy 5:1-2

(POSB: Note 4)

The Purifying Effects of the Gospel

How important is personal purity? If your sin can affect others, then certainly your purity can do the same. The following story illustrates this point:

> Hugh Martin in *The Parables of the Gospels*, tell[s] the story of a rather rough, uncultured man who fell in love with a beautiful vase in a shop window. He bought the vase and put it on the mantelpiece in his room.
>
> There it became a kind of judgment on its surroundings. He had to clean up the room to make it worthy of the vase. The curtains looked dingy beside it. The old chair with the stuffing coming out of the seat would not do. The wallpaper and the paint needed renewing. Gradually the whole room was transformed.[40]

Does your life transform others around you for good? Or is your example one to be avoided?

---

[39] Barry McGee. *Leadership Journal.* Vol. 16, #3, p.38.

[40] O.R. Powell. Cited in: *Encyclopedia of 7,700 Illustrations: Signs of the Times.* Paul Lee Tan, Editor, pp.1105-1106.

Practical Illustrations

10-194

HOLY SPIRIT

2 Timothy 1:13-18

(POSB: Note 2)

The Source of Spiritual Power

How much do you depend upon the power of the Holy Spirit in your life, *every* part of your life? Many people are prone to "help" God out by supplying their own power. And the story has the same ending for all: the power of men will eventually run out.

> There was once a man who developed his entire business through his personality. He was charming, creative, and magnetic. You might even know someone like this. This man had enough charisma and imagination to build several businesses for his self-made empire. He went on for years propelled by his own power, by his extraordinary ability to draw others to him.
>
> One day, the funds to run this man's empire dried up. A recession had devastated the local economy, and in only a few short months every one of his businesses dried up like a vine cut away from its roots. His money and his power had finally run out. His personality no longer paid the bills...and God's power was never even tapped into.

It was the Chinese Christian Watchmen Nee who once said that if the work was spiritual then the supply source would be spiritual as well. In *your* everyday life, which power supply are you plugged into—God's or your own?

❧

10-195

HOPE

1 Timothy 1:1-2

(POSB: Note 1, point 3)

The Power of Hope in Christ

Do you fully understand the power of hope? It is hope in Christ that will carry you through the most desperate trials and temptations of life. Listen to this believer's story.

> I wanted to quit several times. For me, life was losing its meaning and I wanted out. God had given me a test that seemed impossible to pass. In the span of two years I had lost my means of employment, teetered on the edge of divorce, and sank to the depths of despair.
>
> It seemed there was no end to the misery. But in the depths of my heart, a flicker of hope remained as I prayed in faith. I simply refused to believe that Christ would allow me to fall by the wayside. Like a wounded soldier pressing on in the line of fire, my only hope was in Christ. As I prayed and trusted in His ability to redeem my situation, the picture became brighter and brighter.
>
> At first, the circumstances looked worse. Many people around me reminded me of the "friends of Job." But eventually the sovereign mercy and power of God began to take effect: the waters of destruction began to part. In the midst of chaos, God began to put all the pieces of the puzzle together. The job of my greatest desire became available. My marriage was saved and is stronger than ever. Like a prisoner who has

been set free from the fetters of bondage, life is now being *experienced* and *enjoyed* instead of just being *endured.*

Hope will carry you a long way if it is placed in Christ alone.

❧

10-196

HYPOCRISY

1 Timothy 3:1-7

(POSB: Note 2)

Counterfeit Behavior

We easily disqualify ourselves from having a lasting ministry when our behavior contradicts what we say. This minister's example is one of what *not* to do.

Reggie was the kind of man who used smoke and mirrors to hide his character from the members of his congregation. Inside, he struggled with a personal hell everyday. But on the outside, he presented himself as one who had it all together.

He was known for his ability to joke about any topic. One of his favorite jokes was to act effeminate and in a "joking" way give one of his staff members a kiss on the cheek. In a nervous sort of way, everyone would laugh. But in the back of their minds each had serious questions about Reggie's sexual preference. Shocked at even having such notions, the staff would quickly channel their thoughts elsewhere.

Word of Reggie's foolish behavior spread through the church and then the community. His church became the talk of the town. As accusations came, he steadfastly denied each one. And when a television reporter came to inquire, Reggie slammed the door in her face.

As it turns out, Reggie wasn't joking after all. He was a practicing homosexual who *sneaked* out of the closet and tried to keep others in the dark by his coarse jesting. In the end, the joke was on Reggie. His services as minister were no longer needed by the congregation. His ruse destroyed lives and brought shame to the name of Christ. After leaving this congregation behind, he went to a new town and started the whole process all over again.

❧

10-197

HYPOCRISY

2 Timothy 3:10-13

(POSB: Note 3)

Going Beyond Mere Religion

What kinds of things motivate people to join a local church? Well, the right motive is commitment, a commitment to live for Christ. Ken joined his church for all the wrong reasons.

Ken was an attorney who had achieved "success" by the time he was forty years of age. An active member of his political party, he quickly moved up in the ranks and was elected from his district to the state house of representatives.

Being the savvy politician that he was, Ken knew that the key to his political success was to rub elbows with his neighbors. A convenient place to do that was at a large, local church. It was important to his image that his political advertisements stressed both God and family. Being on the membership roll of his church helped him to accomplish his goals.

For Ken, life was pretty predictable until his church sponsored a lay renewal weekend. He tried his best to find other things to do that weekend. But the rain canceled his golf game and his hunting buddy was out of town on business. Ken was left without an excuse. In addition, through a series of ill-fated circumstances, his home was a guest house for the lay visitors. As Ken listened to his guests throughout the weekend, he heard and saw, for the first time in his life, individuals who had a genuine personal relationship with God.

As a result, Ken felt a conflict raging within him, a conflict that forced him to conclude: "I've been playing the game of church, and these people tell me that no one can win the game I'm playing."

There are many people like Ken—impostors who disguise themselves as Christians. Ken was fortunate. God allowed him to see himself as he really was: a sinner in need of a Savior. Ken repented of his sins and Christ came into his heart. What freed Ken? It is simple: he traded in his religion for a relationship with Jesus Christ.

What do you have? Mere religion or a relationship with Christ?

10-198

HYPOCRISY

2 Timothy 3:1-9   **Owning Up to the Truth**

(POSB: Note 3)

One of the greatest deceptions of life is the blanket acceptance of anyone who calls himself a Christian. Many people call themselves Christians, but claiming to be something and actually being it are two entirely different matters. The following story illustrates the point:

A large manufacturing company placed a help-wanted ad in a local newspaper. The ad was written to find qualified applicants with technical experience on a certain kind of machine. The personnel manager's office was swamped with resumes from "qualified" applicants. As the manager opened letter after letter, his heart sank a little bit lower each time. Each resume sang the praises of the applicant's ability to work on this kind of machine. Unfortunately, no such machine existed. The personnel manager was simply performing a test on the reliability of want ads to get the kind of honest employee his company wanted.

The point is this: there are a lot of people who are calling themselves Christians who do not know anything about Christ. God wants real Christians, not fakes. God wants true believers who know *His* power, not their own. God wants a relationship with you, not a life of empty ritual.

PRACTICAL ILLUSTRATIONS

10-199

IDOLATRY

1 Thessalonians 1:5-10

(POSB: Note 4, point 3)

Nail All Your Idols to the Cross

Often, we think in terms of what we want God to be *for us* instead of seeking the only living and true God and finding out what we should be *for Him.* Do you have a story similar to Allen's?

> Like many of us, Allen wanted God to see things his way. Allen was raised in a Christian home, but he allowed different things to become idols in his life, things such as sports heroes, material possessions, and self-seeking adventures. One day, Allen's life came crashing down. His marriage was on the edge of ruin. His children were out of control. His career was heading nowhere fast. Trouble flooded in upon him.
>
> At his wits end, Allen began to seek help. He attended a marriage conference with his wife, and while there he desperately sought the only living and true God. On the final day of the conference, Allen noticed a wooden cross with a simple sign overhead that read: "Jesus invites you to nail every sin to His cross." Hundreds of nails had already been hammered in by others seeking relief from the terrible weight of sin.
>
> With tears rolling down his cheek, Allen walked up and put his nail in the cross alongside the others. As he did, he felt all the hurt, the weight of having lived a life of sin, fall off his shoulders.
>
> "Jesus, I've lived my life for myself. I can't do this alone. Please give me the strength to live for you." After praying, Allen took a deep breath and walked away from the cross that held his sins—every one of them.

Have you turned from God to idols? If so, it is time to nail the idols to the cross and to turn back to God.

❧

10-200

INTEGRITY

1 Thessalonians 5:12-28

(POSB: Note 3, point 7)

Keeping a Pure Witness

In the American Southwest lies the Grand Canyon. Those who have visited this wonder walk away with a lasting impression of its majesty and vastness. Any visitor can walk to its rim and peer down the cliffs without being able to see the bottom. However, this sightseeing is to be done with great caution because there is no rope or rail to protect the curious visitor from falling off the edge to certain death. The smart tourist will draw an imaginary line of safety and stay behind it. With regard to our behavior as believers, we too need to know where to draw the line, when to play it safe, and when to run. Listen to this account:

> Al was a restaurant manager who was handed a wallet lost by one of his customers. To his amazement it contained over a thousand dollars. After taking the wallet to his office, the tempter immediately came and said, "Al, no one would know if *you* took the money. Go ahead...hide the money in your pocket...take that trip that you've always

wanted but couldn't afford...the owner will be glad just to get his credit cards back...he might even give you a reward!"

Despite the great temptation, Al did the right thing. He called the owner of the wallet and told him that everything was in it. After the phone call, he placed it in a safe place until the owner could pick it up.

When the owner of the wallet met with Al, he couldn't thank him enough for his honesty. He had always been skeptical of Christians, but Al's witness planted a deep seed of the gospel in his heart.

With every temptation comes a choice: stay and participate or turn around and run. Which will you choose?

10-201

INTEGRITY

1 Timothy 6:1-2   **Serving Your Employer Faithfully**

(POSB: Note 2)

If you as a believer have a Christian employer, there may be a temptation to take advantage of the situation because of your common faith. This is, of course, completely unfair to the employer. The following example helps illustrate the point.

John was a college student on the dorm's "bowling team"; that is, his job was to clean toilet bowls for an hour and a half once a week. Like most busy people, John was always looking for ways to cut corners and save time. In his eagerness to have time for more fun things, he turned in a false time card.

It did not take John's supervisor long to discover the deception and call John to task. "John, why did you lie about the time you spent on the job?" asked his supervisor, who was a Christian. John was immediately repentant and truly sorry for what he had done. Seeing his change of heart, his supervisor told John to see him the next day to receive his discipline.

Knowing John's desire to become a financial counselor, the supervisor realized how vital integrity was for that kind of work. As he prayed, he came to the conclusion that John's discipline would be to do a study of the word *integrity*. But the basic source for his study had to be the Bible, how the word *integrity* is used in the Bible, and how it applied to John's life.

John took his discipline well. By the end of the year, he was by far the best member of the "bowling team." After graduation, the Lord took a man who understood the meaning of integrity and placed him in a position that required unqualified trust.

If you are ever tempted to cheat or to take unethical shortcuts at work, remember God's challenge to the believer in Ephesians 6:7: "With good will doing service as to the Lord, and not to men."

PRACTICAL ILLUSTRATIONS

10-202

JESUS CHRIST

1 Thessalonians 3:11-13

(POSB: Note 3)

Becoming More Like Christ

Have you ever thought about what life will be like when Christ returns? Sometimes we get so busy that we forget He is preparing us daily to be just like Him. Charles Spurgeon, the great preacher from another generation, had this experience:

> Spurgeon received one day a copy of Andrew Bonar's commentary on Leviticus. Spurgeon was greatly blessed as he read it. He returned it to its author with this request: "Dr. Bonar, please autograph this book, and paste your picture on the title page. Then return it to me."
>
> Bonar did as requested. Below the picture he wrote, "Dear Spurgeon: Here is the book with my autograph and my photograph. If you had been willing to wait a short season you could have had a better picture. When I see Christ, I shall be like Him."[41]

If you are a Christian believer, take heart—God is working in you to make you more and more like Him every day!

❧

10-203

JESUS CHRIST

2 Thessalonians 2:13-17

(POSB: Note 5)

Christ: The Secret to Your Salvation

The secret to your salvation is in your Savior. In Christ, you find every resource for salvation. This truth was captured during a hurricane in the Gulf of Mexico.

> A news report highlighted a rescue device used on the oil rigs. In case of fire or (in this case) hurricane, rig workers scramble into the bullet shaped "bus" and strap themselves into their seats. When the entry port is shut, the vehicle is released down a chute and projected away from the rig. The seat belts protect the occupants from the impact with the water. The capsule then bobs in the sea until the rescuers come to pick it up.
>
> The device parallels the theological truth of Romans 8:1—"Therefore, there is now no condemnation for those who are **in** Christ Jesus."
>
> Justification does not mean our world always stops falling apart. The rig still may topple in the hurricane. But those in the right place, whether a rescue module or spiritually in Christ, are saved from the ultimate consequences of the storm. The storm will take its course. The welfare of the workers depends on whether they are *in* the rescue device.[42]

❧

---

[41] Walter B. Knight. *Knight's Treasury of 2,000 Illustrations*, p.352.

[42] Craig B. Larson, Editor. *Illustrations for Preaching & Teaching*, p.213.

72

PRACTICAL ILLUSTRATIONS

10-204

JESUS CHRIST
2 Timothy 2:8-13
(POSB: Introduction)

Jesus Christ: The Resurrected Lord

In the 1960's some people followed an unorthodox teaching that proclaimed, "God is dead." God's tragic demise left man alone to fend for himself—which was just fine with some people. For if God were dead, then man would be in control and could live as he wanted, doing his own thing. Man would become his own god (a philosophy known as humanism).

However, history has proven that when man assumes to be god, the gospel is transformed from "good news" to "ghastly news." Fortunately, God is not dead. He is alive! And because He lives, His gospel has the power to save a depraved humanity, one person at a time.

One of the most important charges ever given to believers is to remember the gospel: Jesus Christ was raised from the dead and is the resurrected Lord. How important is it to you that you have a resurrected Lord? Your answer determines where you will spend eternity!

10-205

JUDGING
1 Timothy 5:21-25
(POSB: Note 5)

Does God Need Help?

Some Christians appear to be "gifted" with judging the faults of others. Those who do so usually do and say the most foolish things. The following story illustrates this point:

> John Killinger tells about the manager of a minor league baseball team who was so disgusted with his center fielder's performance that he ordered him to the dugout and assumed the position himself. The first ball that came into center field took a bad hop and hit the manager in the mouth. The next one was a high fly ball, which he lost in the glare of the sun—until it bounced off his forehead. The third was a hard line drive that he charged with outstretched arms; unfortunately, it flew between his hands and smacked his eye.
>
> Furious, he ran back to the dugout, grabbed the center fielder by the uniform, and shouted, "You idiot! You've got center field so messed up that even I can't do a thing with it!"[43]

When you assume God needs your help in judging others, you put yourself in a position to be judged!

---

[43] Craig B. Larson, Editor. *Illustrations for Preaching & Teaching,* p.16.

PRACTICAL ILLUSTRATIONS

10-206

JUDGMENT

2 Thessalonians 1:6-12
Escaping Judgment
(POSB: Note 6)

Thankfully, God has made a way to escape eternal judgment. Tom M. Olson, in *Now*, illustrates with this striking point:

> A Christian, as he entered a barber shop, heard a man say, "I was born a sinner. It was no responsibility of mine. It would, therefore, be unjust for God to judge or condemn me for that in which I had no responsibility whatever, no matter what the Bible or preachers say!" The Christian pointed out that the Bible does not say God will condemn us because we are born sinners, but that He will do so if we remain sinners, rejecting the Savior, by whom He has opened the way of escape for us.
>
> He used this illustration: "Suppose someone has occasion to pass your door at midnight, and notices that fire has broken out in your house. You are asleep, unaware of the danger you are in; the alarm is given and you are awakened. In this circumstance, what would your responsibility be?" "Well," the man answered, "surely I would be responsible to heed the warning and escape as quickly as possible." "But supposing you were to answer the one who warned you, 'I didn't set this building on fire, and have no responsibility for it,' and so remain in the house. What then?" "In that case," he said, "I would be a fool, and responsible if I lost my life."[44]

There is a raging fire in the household of mankind. Have you found the Fire Escape?

❧

10-207

JUDGMENT

2 Thessalonians 2:1-3
Judgment Day: Truth or Fiction?
(POSB: Introduction)

Have you ever seen a man walking down a street holding a sign that says: "Repent! Judgment is near!"?

The majority of people do not take that message very seriously these days. The man is pictured as rather eccentric and out of touch with reality. But is the day of the Lord to be taken seriously? Yes, it is. What, then, does the Bible say about the day of the Lord?

When the Bible refers to *the day of Christ* or *the day of the Lord*, it does not mean a single day in history. It is using the word *day* in a forceful or emphatic sense just as men do when they speak of the great day of space exploration or the great day of some world leader or the great day of creation. The day of the Lord covers a long span of time and some very significant events. In the Bible it covers the span of history from the coming of Christ to the end of time. It will be a terrible time of trouble, a time that is known as that great and terrible day of judgment, the day when the wrath

---

[44] Walter B. Knight. *Knight's Treasury of 2,000 Illustrations*, p.192.

of God will fall upon all the meanness, viciousness, ugliness, and filthiness of men. However, note this important point: no believer has to fear the day of the Lord. The day of the Lord launches God's judgment against unbelievers; it is not the judgment of believers.

❧

10-208

Judgment

2 Thessalonians 1:6-12   **Reverence for the Judge**

(POSB: Introduction)

Have you ever had to stand before a judge for sentencing? Hopefully not. But if you did, you found yourself at the mercy of the official. If you were found guilty of breaking the law, the judge had the right to place the full weight of the law—and its punishment—upon you. The possibility of this happening is a deterrent to most people and prevents *them* from pursuing lives of crime. They do not want to face a judge's wrath, so they choose to live on the right side of the law. A healthy fear of judgment keeps them straight.

A wise man lives lawfully to avoid judgment by an earthly judge. An even wiser man lives righteously to avoid judgment by the King of kings and Lord of lords.

"The fear of the Lord is the beginning of wisdom" (Ps.111:10).

❧

10-209

Law, The

Titus 3:1-2   **Protection, Not Restriction**

(POSB: Note 1)

What would your community be like if the civil laws were not enforced? It is not hard to imagine the chaos that would develop—the pain that would be experienced—if *you* were above the law. God has a very good reason for telling His children to obey the laws of the community. Timothy Munyon writes:

> While living in Florida, I had several friends who worked cleaning rooms at a nationally known inn located directly on the white sands of the Gulf of Mexico. They spent their work breaks running barefoot in the sand. The problem was the inn required all employees to wear shoes at all times while working. I noticed the employees responded in one of two ways.
>
> The majority thought the rule restricted their freedom. The rooms had shag carpeting, delightful to the bare toes, and just a few steps away lay the beach. To them the rule to wear shoes was nothing more than employer harassment.
>
> But a minority of the employees looked at the rule differently. Sometimes late night parties would...[leave] small pieces of broken glass. Occasionally a stickpin would be found hidden in the deep shag piles. Some knew the pain of skinning bare toes on the steel bed frame while making a bed. This minority saw the rule as protection, not restriction.[45]

---

[45] Craig B. Larson, Editor. *Illustrations for Preaching & Teaching.* From the *Letter to Diognetus*, p.126.

PRACTICAL ILLUSTRATIONS

And so it is with believers. Those who choose to disobey the laws will suffer the pain and consequences. Those who choose to abide by the laws will enjoy God's protection and approval. To rebel against the laws of your community (those laws that do not contradict God's law) is to rebel against God Himself.

🐚

10-210

LAWLESSNESS

2 Thessalonians 2:4-9

(POSB: Note 3, point 2)

Without Moral Leadership

One day in the future, lawlessness will be allowed to run rampant, without moral direction. Contrast that day to a day years ago in the nation of Malaysia, where a cross-country race was held. Several hours after the starter's pistol was fired, none of the competitors had crossed the finish line. Fearing the worst, the race's officials got into their automobiles to search for the missing runners. Their fears were soon laid to rest. It turns out that the lead runner had taken a wrong turn and the rest of the pack had followed him for at least a ten-mile jaunt. All of the runners were sprinting in the wrong direction!

The world will one day find itself in the same situation. The Holy Spirit will step aside as the antichrist leads the lost into a race of lawlessness with absolutely no moral direction. Evil will become indescribable as it leaves morality behind in the dust. When the restraining power of God is removed from the earth, be careful whose lead you follow!

🐚

10-211

LEADERSHIP

1 Timothy 3:1-7

(POSB: Introduction)

Ask God for Church Leaders

Do you feel comfortable entrusting your soul to the care of your church leaders? The Bible instructs us to...

"Obey them that have the rule over you, and submit yourselves: for they watch for your souls, as they that must give account, that they may do it with joy, and not with grief: for that is unprofitable for you" (Hebrews 13:17).

One of the most important duties of the local church is to ask God for leaders who qualify according to the Scripture. A church that ignores God's criteria for ministers or elders and accepts leaders due to popularity or politics defiles the office of the elder. Woe to any body of believers who compromise on this issue.

🐚

PRACTICAL ILLUSTRATIONS

10-212

LIFESTYLE

1 Thessalonians 1:5-10   **Imitate the Lord**

(POSB: Note 2)

The word *follow* means to imitate. Is it right for people to imitate and follow preachers and other outstanding Christian leaders? A.T. Robertson gives an excellent answer to the question:

> It is a daring thing to expect people to "imitate" the preacher, but Paul adds "and of the Lord," for he only expected or desired "imitation" as he himself imitated the Lord Jesus, as he expressly says in 1 Cor. 11:1. The peril of it all is that people so easily and so readily imitate the preacher when he does not imitate the Lord.[46]

∽ঔ

10-213

LIFESTYLE

Philemon 1-7   **Life on Earth Is Limited**

(POSB: Introduction)

When you die, what kinds of things will be said about you? What will people remember? Just think. Year after year you walk through life—encountering thousands and thousands of experiences. But when your life ends, someone will summarize your life in one or two paragraphs of the obituary column. If you were to die today, what would be written in your paragraph? How would someone sum up your life? Now, think in even more precise terms. What will be written on your headstone?

Almost everyone desires to be remembered as someone who has made a significant contribution to the human race. But remember this important fact: once you die, you can accomplish no more. Your legacy is being chiseled now into the granite memories of those around you. The choices you make day by day will ultimately be a part of your legacy. Your lifestyle will reflect whether you have served Christ with all your heart—or served yourself.

∽ঔ

10-214

LIFESTYLE

1 Thessalonians 5:12-28   **Living Expectantly for Christ's Return**

(POSB: Introduction)

If Jesus were to return this week, would He find you in a place pleasing to Him?

> One time a man went to a movie at the local theater with several friends. This movie was the talk of Hollywood and a recipient of several awards. There was just one problem—the movie was anything but nurturing to his spirit. As he sat in the theater, he justified his attendance by the fact that he liked one of the actors. But settling into his seat, he began to fidget and become disturbed by what he saw on the silver screen.

---

[46] A.T. Robertson. *Word Pictures in the New Testament*, Vol.4. (Nashville, TN: Broadman Press, 1931), p.11.

PRACTICAL ILLUSTRATIONS

He had a decision to make: To go or to stay. To go would mean being ridiculed by his friends. He would also have wasted his money, he reasoned. But to stay would mean quenching the Holy Spirit. As he struggled to make his decision, this inescapable thought filled his mind, "If Jesus came back today, would He want to find me here?" "Enough said," he thought, and got up out of his seat. Praise God, he won that battle.

But on another occasion, he began watching a questionable TV program. He had to make the same decision all over again.

- Should he switch channels?
- Should he turn the TV off?
- Should he continue watching and grieve God's Holy Spirit?

The problem was not the random attacks of Satan. Instead, the behavior of the man needed to be changed. If there is one thing that will change our behavior, it is seeing and grasping the reality of the Lord's return to earth. If a person really believes that Jesus Christ is returning to earth, it will radically change his life.

10-215

LIFESTYLE

1 Timothy 6:1-2

Your Witness at Work

(POSB: Introduction)

How real is your Christian witness at work? Should your witness even be evident in a secular setting? In many cases, a believer's witness is most powerful when it permeates the workplace. Remember, the best sermons are the ones that are *seen*, not heard. The Christian believer must, therefore, be a diligent worker and be on his best behavior at work, respecting and obeying what his employer says and requires. He must be appreciative for having work to do.

The instructions to slaves and masters in the New Testament are applicable to every generation of workmen. As Francis Foulkes says, "...the principles of the whole section apply to employees and employers in every age, whether in the home, in business, or in the state."[47]

What impact or impression are you making on your employer and your co-workers?

10-216

LOVE

Philemon 1-7

A Life Marked with Love

(POSB: Note 5)

The language of love is best understood when Christians demonstrate Christ-like care. See how one missionary's life touched the needs of the people around him.

---

[47] Francis Foulkes. *The Epistle of Paul to the Ephesians.* "Tyndale New Testament Commentaries." (Grand Rapids, MI: Eerdmans Publishing Company, n.d.), p.167.

PRACTICAL ILLUSTRATIONS

A missionary in New Guinea returned [home] after several years of service. His friend said to him, "Jones, tell me what you found at your station in New Guinea?"

"Found! I found something that looked more hopeless than if I had been sent into the jungle to a lot of tigers."

"What do you mean?"

"Why those people were so degraded that they seemed utterly devoid of moral sense. They were worse than beasts. If a mother were carrying her little baby, and the baby began to cry, she would throw it into the ditch and let it die. If a man saw his father break his leg, he would leave him upon the roadside to die. They had no compassion whatever. They did not know what it meant."

"Well, what did you do for people like that? Did you preach to them?"

"Preach? No! I lived."

"Lived? How did you live?"

"When I saw a baby crying, I picked it up and comforted it. When I saw a man with a broken leg, I mended it. When I saw people in distress, I took them in and pitied them. I took care of them. I lived that way. And those people began to come to me and say: 'What does this mean? What are you doing this for?' Then I had my chance and I preached the gospel."

"Did you succeed?"

"When I left, I left a church!"[48]

How are you showing your love for others day by day?

10-217

LOVE

1 Thessalonians 4:9-12

(POSB: Note 1)

Teaching to Love

Scripture declares a simple but clear command: believers are to love one another as brothers and sisters in Christ. We are foolish to think that we can excuse or exempt ourselves from God's teaching.

Years ago, a church family fell between the cracks of Christian care. The breadwinner had lost his job and for nine months was out of work. He mailed resumes out across the country, but to no avail.

During this difficult time, the leaders of their church failed to reach out to them. Because of the church's inaction and their inability to demonstrate love, this family teetered on the edge of both financial and spiritual ruin. It was only the grace of God that kept them from total despair.

What happened to this family is not unique at all. You may even know a family like this. The problem is that many people equate spiritual leadership with spiritual maturity. But just because people are leaders in the church, it cannot be assumed that they know how to love those in need. More often than not, people do not love because they were never taught how to love.

---

[48] *Record of Christian Work.* Walter B. Knight. *Knight's Master Book of 4,000 Illustrations*, pp.618-619.

Look at your own church: if the leaders are ministering in love, the followers will do the same. If you were in trouble, would your church, your leaders, your brothers and sisters in Christ reach out in love to help you?

❦

10-218

LOVE

1 Thessalonians 2:1-12   **TLC Goes a Long Way**

(POSB: Note 7)

Are you noted for the amount of "TLC" (tender-loving-care) that you shower on those around you? Listen to this touching story from the foreign mission field:

> Rev. Ira Gillett, missionary to Portuguese East Africa, tells the story of a group of natives who made a long journey and walked past a government hospital to come to the mission hospital for treatment. When asked why they had walked the extra distance to reach the mission hospital when the same medicines were available at the government institution, they replied, "The medicines may be the same, but the hands are different."[49]

The servants of our Lord must be gentle, caring, sincere. Can the same be said about you?

❦

10-219

LOVE

1 Thessalonians 3:11-13   **The World's Greatest Virtue**

(POSB: Introduction)

When you think of your neighbors, your co-workers, strangers, even enemies—do you think in terms of loving them? How you answer this question is a strong indicator of how mature your love is for God. There are some who feel that God's love is reserved for the "lovely"—those who are easy to love—that anyone who falls outside of that invisible line does not deserve to be loved by God nor by His people. But is God's love that limited in scope? Certainly not! Remember: "For God so loved the **world**." God's love flows over the walls that some people build and floods the souls of the lost with His mercy.

It is God's love that is to make the Christian believer distinctive from the rest of the people in the world.

The greatest virtue in the world is love. This is the one possession that man must have if he is to have an abundant life. Without love, man is nothing.

---

[49] *Upper Room.* Walter B. Knight. *3,000 Illustrations for Christian Service*, p.402.

PRACTICAL ILLUSTRATIONS

10-220

LUST

2 Timothy 2:22-26

(POSB: Note 1)

The Consequences of Lust

The charge is clear: flee the youthful lusts of the world. Young and old—all of you—flee the lusts that are common to young men and women. Does this really mean what it says? What if you choose to flee from the Lord and follow these lusts? Can you expect any negative consequences? Yes!

> When Leonardo da Vinci was painting his masterpiece, "The Last Supper," he sought long for a model for his Christ. At last he located a chorister [a choir boy] in one of the churches of Rome who was lovely in life and features, a young man named Pietro Bandinelli.
>
> Years passed, and the painting was still unfinished. All the disciples had been portrayed save one—Judas Iscariot. Now he started to find a man whose face was hardened and distorted by sin—and at last he found a beggar on the streets of Rome with a face so villainous, he shuddered when he looked at him. He hired the man to sit for him as he painted the face of Judas on his canvas. When he was about to dismiss the man, he said, "I have not yet found out your name." "I am Pietro Bandinelli," he replied, "I also sat for you as your model of Christ."[50]

If you were given a chair in da Vinci's painting, in whose place would you be sitting today—Judas' or Jesus'? The path you choose to travel in life determines which place you will end up.

❧

10-221

MATERIALISM

1 Timothy 6:6-10

(POSB: Note 1)

How Much Is Enough?

A popular American expression speaks of "keeping up with the Joneses," that is, having as many material possessions as your neighbors. In the race to see who can outdo whom, contentment is becoming extinct even in the lives of many Christians. See if you can find yourself in this amusing story.

> As a new family was moving in across the street, an observant neighbor was struck by the amount of things one family could accumulate. The stream of boxes unloaded from the moving van was seemingly endless. Their four cars were parked on the lawn out of the way. The new family lived by the popular adage, "If you've got it, flaunt it." He couldn't be sure, but he thought he counted at least five television sets unloaded and taken into the house. "Maybe they have a few spare ones in case one breaks," he thought to himself.

---

[50] *Indian Christian.* Paul Lee Tan. *Encyclopedia of 7,700 Illustrations: Signs of the Times*, p.1286.

PRACTICAL ILLUSTRATIONS

Despite all the commotion, the man decided to go and greet his new neighbor. "Hi there! Good to meet you." While pointing to the moving van, he remarked, "Do you think all of your stuff is going to fit into the house?" With a sense of pride, the new neighbor responded, "I doubt it. I've just got too much. If you ever need to borrow anything, let me know—I'm sure to have it."

Thinking to himself he could use some of the items, the old neighbor responded pointedly, "If you need help getting rid of some things, I'll be glad to take them off your hands."

Both of these men, in their own way, were focusing on the material. But material things cannot give anyone contentment—not permanently, not perfectly. It is through God and God alone that man finds a contentment that leaves him wanting for nothing.

10-222

MEEKNESS

Titus 3:1-2   **Humbly Serving in the Strength of the Lord**

(POSB: Note 6)

Some people think of themselves as God's gift to the world. However, a meek person is not this way at all. Listen carefully to this story about an American general.

General Grant was stricken with a fatal illness. As he approached the end of his life, he felt his need of the Saviour and His sustaining presence. He called for a minister. Simply the minister presented the gospel to him. "General," he said, "God in love sent the Saviour to seek and to save that which was lost. If you will sincerely call upon Him from your heart, you will receive from Him mercy and abundant pardon!"

When the minister knelt and prayed, God opened the heart of the general and he was joyfully converted. God cleansed his heart from sin. The minister was elated. "God's kingdom has gained a great acquisition in your conversion, General," said the minister.

Immediately General Grant protested, saying, "God does not need great men, but great men need God! There is just one thing that I now greatly desire since Christ's great peace has come to me..." "What's that, General?" asked the minister. "I would like to live one year more so that I might tell others of this wonderful gift of God's love!"[51]

Strength is always found in true meekness. Meekness is not weakness; rather it is the proper way to demonstrate strength and resolve.

---

[51] Walter B. Knight. *Knight's Treasury of 2,000 Illustrations*, p.434.

PRACTICAL ILLUSTRATIONS

10-223

MERCY

1 Timothy 1:1-2

(POSB: Note 2)

Undeserved, But Freely Given

Is mercy a part of your life? Is it something you practice daily? The following story is a striking example of someone changed by mercy.

Like many young married couples, Dan and Tracy went into their marriage without understanding money management. It did not take them long to go from debt-free to debt-ridden. A combination of bad advice, unplanned hospital bills, and bad circumstances left them trapped, never having enough money. Month after month they fell further and further into debt.

As the pressure increased, Dan prayed one of those "I'll pray, but it will do no good" kind of prayers. He said, "Lord, I know we do not deserve a second chance, but we've learned so much about good stewardship and what not to do, I'd love to start all over again." In a whispered hush, he said "Amen."

Sometime later, Dan and Tracy shared with their pastor their desire to get their finances in order. The pastor sensed their sincerity and wanted to help them overcome their crushing debt. But how?

Expecting harsh condemnation for being such poor stewards, Dan and Tracy were shocked at the mercy extended to them by the pastor. Two weeks later, another group of Christians got involved in Dan and Tracy's life. These unnamed Christian businessmen had started a ministry to help couples just like them. The burden of the businessmen was to supply funds at no interest to Christians who were in need—as long as the couples would...

- agree to live by a budget
- repay the loan so others could benefit from their ministry
- no longer use credit cards

As Dan signed the needed paperwork, his earlier prayer came back to mind. "Lord, You are so merciful. I deserved condemnation, but You provided mercy."

How can you provide mercy to someone in need today?

10-224

MINISTRY

2 Timothy 4:1-5

(POSB: Note 4, point 4)

Are You Fulfilling Your Ministry?

As a believer, how much of an effort do you make to fulfill your ministry on earth? Do you even know what your ministry is? Do you do just enough to get by with or do you pour yourself into it?

The story is told of three men who died and went to heaven. During their processing by Saint Peter, the first man pulled out his resume and said, "I've got a seminary
degree, and I've brought my sharpest three-piece suit to be presented to God. I'm sure you folks have a special place for me to serve." Peter looked at his records and saw

83

that the man was more interested in style than in substance. "End of the line please. We'll process you later."

The next man conducted his ministry according to the following standards: "My ministry will be done when it is convenient for me, when it doesn't interfere with other important things in my life." His standards seemed to serve him well. He lived his life for himself and had plenty of time for pleasure. Peter looked at his records again, rolled his eyes and said, "I'm sorry. Please stand in the Wasted Rewards line."

The third man did not look very impressive. In fact, he looked haggard. He had spent a great deal of energy caring for other people. Ministering to others in the name of Jesus Christ wore him out. However, he had only one regret: he could not get to everybody. Peter greeted him warmly and said, "Brother, please go on ahead. You have fulfilled your ministry on earth. Enter into the rest of our Lord. Well done, faithful servant!"

One day you too will stand face-to-face with the Lord Jesus Christ, the Son of God Himself. Will He be able to say to you, "Well done, good and faithful servant"?

❧

10-225

MINISTRY

2 Timothy 4:9-22   **Keeping Your Focus**

(POSB: Introduction)

It is not how you start a race that is really important but how you finish it. The pages of history are littered with the names of men and women who started toward a specific goal but never reached their mark. Many allowed pride to keep them from finishing. Others allowed tragic circumstances to knock them off course. Still more just lost sight of their goal, which happens quite easily when concentration is lost. The following story illustrates the point:

Every now and then losing sight of the goal happens on the football field. Years ago during a college football game, an excited young man recovered a fumbled football and began to run as hard as he could. He zigged and he zagged while avoiding the desperate attempts of the opposing players who were trying to tackle him. As he continued to elude the players on the other team, he began to notice something very strange. His own teammates were also a part of the chase to tackle him! "Why are my own teammates trying to tackle me?" he asked himself. As he ran down the sidelines, his coach, whose face was beat red, yelled to him, "Turn around! You're going the wrong way!" What was important to that coach was not that his player had the ball, nor that his player had a lot of energy, nor that he was running toward a goal. What was important to this wayward player's coach was that he was running toward the wrong goal. Nothing else that he did mattered. Once the player came to his senses, he came to an abrupt halt. He turned around and headed back in the right direction—with one thing in mind: finishing his run by crossing the right goal.

For every Christian believer, this life is just the beginning. Eternity awaits.

❧

PRACTICAL ILLUSTRATIONS

10-226

MONEY

1 Timothy 6:6-10

(POSB: Note 2)

Deadly Greed

If someone offered you a sack of gold, would you take it? Before you answer too quickly, listen to this story and then give your answer.

"The voyage home to Spain has been a long time coming, but after a very successful gold strike in the New World, it is time to cash in on our good fortune," thought Carlos, the ship's captain, as he relaxed on the deck of his ship. Sitting there, Carlos imagined what he would do with his share of the treasure. But then off in the distance he saw dark clouds rising over the horizon.

Carlos and his crew had made the trans-Atlantic trip several times and were considered to be sea-worthy sailors. But this time, they sailed into the storm of the century. They had never seen waves like the ones that rocked their ship back and forth. As the water flooded the hold, Carlos gave the order to throw everything of significant weight overboard.

With hearts heavier than their gold fortune, they began to throw bags of gold overboard. It was to no avail. The ship continued to sink. The captain ordered the men to lower lifeboats and to abandon the ship. During all of the confusion, one of the sailors took a bag of gold and stuffed it in his shirt. "Those poor suckers. They've lost everything," he thought to himself.

Yet as he stepped into the lifeboat, he was thrown off balance and fell into the angry sea. "Swim to us!" shouted his shipmates. But the weight of the gold pulled the man under, never to be seen again. The sailor's greed formed his grave, one that showed no respect for the material possessions.

Is the love of the world dragging you down? Let it go. Let the Savior rescue you before it is too late.

❧

10-227

MONEY

1 Timothy 6:17-21

(POSB: Note 1, point 5)

God's Purpose for Man's Money

There is no question that God allows certain believers to become materially rich. However, it is never for their gain; it is always for the gain of His Kingdom. Here is an inspiring example of channeling God's resources to do God's work.

Mr. Wilson was a successful businessman in the orange juice business. He was on the cutting edge of the production, shipping, and marketing of his product. In fact, he was so successful that he became a dominant player in the juice industry.

From humble beginnings, he became a very rich man. Mr. Wilson was never one to count his money except for the purpose of giving to the work of God. He tithed and gave huge sums to help meet the ministry and building needs of his church. In addition, he was led by the Lord to become involved in financing a Bible college. He helped the college build its buildings, but he also did something that every student at the Bible college appreciated: provided free orange juice for breakfast through his company.

When Mr. Wilson visited the campus, he had breakfast in the cafeteria that *he* had provided, had a glass of juice that *he* had paid for, sat with a student body that *he* had provided with scholarships; but he was never recognized by anyone. But for Mr. Wilson, that was acceptable. Recognition was not his motivation. He gave because God had gripped his heart. He gave out of thanksgiving for God's salvation. And because God saved him, Mr. Wilson invested in the lives of people, people who would take the gospel, the good news, to the nations of the earth.

No matter how much or how little you have, are you using God's blessings to further God's Kingdom or your own?

10-228

OBEDIENCE

2 Thessalonians 1:6-12

(POSB: Note 3)

Know the Language of Obedience

Every professing Christian needs to be sure—absolutely sure—that his profession is genuine. The alternative is that he will appear before Christ with a false profession. A tragic moment pulled from the pages of history illustrates this fact.

In July 1976, Israeli commandos made a daring raid at an airport in Entebbe, Uganda, in which 103 Jewish hostages were freed. In less than 15 minutes, the soldiers had killed all seven kidnappers and set the captives free.

As successful as the rescue was, however, three of the hostages were killed during the raid. As the commandos entered the terminal, they shouted in Hebrew, "Get down! Crawl!" The Jewish hostages understood and lay down on the floor, while the guerrillas, who did not speak Hebrew, were left standing. Quickly the rescuers shot the upright kidnappers.

But two of the hostages hesitated—perhaps to see what was happening—and were also cut down. One young man was lying down and actually stood up when the commandos entered the airport. He, too, was shot with the bullets meant for the enemy. Had these three heeded the soldier's command, they would have been freed with the rest of the captives.

Salvation is open to all, but we must heed Christ's command to repent and make Him Lord. Otherwise, we will perish with the judgment meant for the Enemy.[52]

You do not need to be fluent in Hebrew, but it will be to your great gain to know the language of obedience.

---

[52] Craig B. Larson, Editor. *Illustrations for Preaching & Teaching*, p.168.

PRACTICAL ILLUSTRATIONS

10-229

OBEDIENCE

2 Timothy 2:22-26

(POSB: Introduction)

The Need to Follow Instructions

How good are you at following instructions? Hopefully better than the student in this story:

> John really prided himself on quickly completing exams. One day an exam began with these simple instructions: "Read through the entire exam first before answering any questions." But quickly proceeding to work through each question, John ignored the instruction. He was soon astonished to see several classmates getting up and turning in their exams. "Apparently, they didn't study for this exam like I did," he concluded.
>
> An hour later, he found himself alone, finishing up the exam. When he finally got to the last question, it read: "Do not answer any questions on this exam. Just write your name at the top of the page and turn it in!"
>
> The student's heart sank. He had failed, because he would not follow simple instructions.

People who fail to follow God's instructions will fail a lot more than just an exam—they will fail at life.

~~

10-230

OUTREACH

Titus 1:5-9

(POSB: Note 1)

The Great Danger of Complacency

Would you consider your church to be growing in Christ? Here is a story of a church that lost its vision.

> An evangelical church found its membership shrinking with age. It did not take many years for the church to turn from one of relevance to one of indifference.
>
> What happened? Just this: the members of the congregation had become satisfied with the way things were. They became complacent and self-centered. They just didn't care about people around them. Two or three powerful families were the self-appointed holy guardians of the gate to the church. Eventually, their pastor of ten years gave up and resigned.

If a church does not reach beyond it own walls, it will simply rot from within. Are you doing your part to keep your church alive?

~~

10-231

OUTREACH

Philemon 8-21

(POSB: Note 5)

Love Your Church Family

The role of the church is not to become a selective club of religious snobs. The warmth of God's fellowship was never meant to be excluded from those outside the cliques within the church.

Man-made barriers should never hinder us from reaching out and receiving other people who are different. The love of God compels us to lay down our lives for one another.

In the December 31, 1989 *Chicago Tribune*, the editors printed their photos of the decade. One of them...captured a grim fireman and paramedic carrying a fire victim away from the scene. The blaze, which happened in Chicago in December 1984, at first seemed routine. But then firefighters discovered the bodies of a mother and five children huddled in the kitchen of an apartment....The firefighters surmised, "She could have escaped with two or three of the children but couldn't decide whom to pick. She chose to wait with all of them for the firefighters to arrive. All of them died of smoke inhalation."

There are times when you just don't leave those you love.[53]

You just don't leave someone because...
- he is poorer than you
- he is richer than you
- he is from another culture
- his skin color is different
- he speaks with a different accent or language
- he has a dark or shameful past
- he looks different
- he acts different
- you are forced to choose between being popular or being shunned

The Christian believer who really cares will make a special effort to break down the walls that divide people, not turn people away and leave them. If you truly love people, you embrace them and welcome them into the fellowship of God's people and church.

---

[53] Craig B. Larson. *Illustrations for Preaching and Teaching*, p.145.

PRACTICAL ILLUSTRATIONS

10-232

PERSEVERANCE

2 Timothy 1:13-18

(POSB: Introduction)

Hold Fast to the Lord Jesus

How strong is your grip? When you shake someone's hand...when you hold a tennis racket...when you hold a tool? Whether it be a handshake, participation in sports, or being a handyman around the home, a firm grip is desirable. Just think how limp a weak handshake feels. A bad grip on a tennis racket will propel the racket out of your hand and into the air. A weak grip on a hammer will not drive the nail into the board. Just as it is important to have a strong grip in these areas, it is critically important for the Christian believer to have a good grip on the Lord Jesus.

The Psalmist, King David, reminds us with this vivid illustration:

> "My soul clings to Thee; Thy right hand upholds me" (Psalm 63:8, NASB).

In other words, "Hang on as He holds on to you!" In a world that is filled with wickedness and false teaching, believers must hold fast to the Lord Jesus Christ.

10-233

PERSEVERANCE

2 Timothy 2:1-7

(POSB: Note 5)

Rely on God's Strength

Do you ever feel like just quitting and giving up? Do you get so tired that you feel you cannot go another step? The Christian believer is not immune to these feelings, but the challenge is to persevere through them. For example...

The folklore surrounding Poland's famous concert pianist and prime minister, Ignace Paderewski, includes this story:

A mother, wishing to encourage her young son's progress at the piano, bought tickets for a Paderewski performance. When the night arrived, they found their seats near the front of the concert hall and eyed the majestic Steinway waiting on stage.

Soon the mother found a friend to talk to, and the boy slipped away. When eight o'clock arrived, the spotlights came on, the audience quieted, and only then did they notice the boy up on the bench, innocently picking out "Twinkle, Twinkle, Little Star."

His mother gasped, but before she could retrieve her son, the master appeared on the stage and quickly moved to the keyboard.

"Don't quit—keep playing," he whispered to the boy. Leaning over, Paderewski reached down with his left hand and began filling in a bass part. Soon his right arm reached around the other side, encircling the child, to add a running obbligato. Together, the old master and the young novice held the crowd mesmerized.[54]

---

[54] Craig B. Larson, Editor. *Illustrations for Preaching & Teaching*, p.221.

PRACTICAL ILLUSTRATIONS

Serving the Lord is hard work. Using your own strength will exhaust you and you will be tempted to quit. But using God's strength as you work hard will produce beautiful music.

❧

10-234

PERSEVERANCE

2 Timothy 3:10-13

(POSB: Note 2)

A Visible Mark of Godliness

Suffering will seldom be a popular option for anyone. In many cultures, persecution is primarily verbal and mental; but in numerous cultures, persecution is physical. In either case, perseverance is a visible mark of godliness.

> Some years ago Japan took over Korea. Many of the leading Christians were bitterly persecuted. Some were imprisoned in Japanese jails. Those who were not persecuted felt that they were somehow lacking in their Christianity.
> A native Methodist pastor went to a missionary and said, "Maksa, there must be something wrong with us Methodists. I fear that we are not living as godly as we ought to live. There are thirty-seven Presbyterians in jail and only one Methodist! Does not the Lord count us 'worthy to suffer shame for His name?'"[55]

We too should expect to suffer for being followers of Christ—He has told us that we *will* suffer. Be sure you are prepared for the inevitable, that you will be counted *worthy* to suffer shame for His name.

❧

10-235

PERSPECTIVE

2 Timothy 2:1-7

(POSB: Note 6)

Understanding Through Doing

Does it ever seem like your memory is gone, like nothing seems to stick? God's Word has a cure for your lapse of memory. Through review and prayer, God will help you remember what you have heard. Understanding will come if you pay attention. Listen to this conversation between a student and his teacher.

> "Why was it that so few understood Jesus?" the student asked the Teacher. "The Pharisees and scribes constantly opposed him. His disciples often seemed confused by his teaching, and still others suggested that he was possessed with demons. Even his own family feared for his mental health."
> The Teacher replied, "Once there was a wedding couple who brought in the finest fiddlers and banjo players to entertain their guests immediately after the ceremony. The music was so captivating that soon everyone, young and old alike, began to dance. The people flung their bodies first one way and then another. The church was filled with joy.

---

[55] Walter B. Knight. *Knight's Treasury of 2,000 Illustrations*, p.261.

PRACTICAL ILLUSTRATIONS

"Two men drove by the church building in their new luxury automobile with the windows of the sedan rolled up and loud music blaring from their car radio. They could not hear a single sound from the outside of the automobile. When they saw people jumping around they stopped the car, shaking their heads at the sight. 'What a bunch of weirdoes,' the driver said to his companion. 'See how they fling themselves about. I tell you the folks that go to that church are crazy.'"

The Teacher paused after finishing his story. "That is the conclusion people draw when they cannot hear the music to which others are dancing."[56]

The only way to understand what the Lord is doing in His church is to be *in* His church. Are you looking from the outside in or from the inside out?

10-236

PRAISE

1 Timothy 1:12-17

(*POSB: Note 3*)

The Sound of Genuine Praise

The only legitimate response from a sinner who is saved by grace is this: unreserved praise for the eternal King of glory. Your praise is to rise from a changed heart.

A story is told in which a man went to church with an angel as his guide. Every seat in the church was filled, but there was something strange about it all. The organist moved his fingers over the keys but no music came forth from the pipes. The choir arose to sing, and their lips moved, but not a sound was to be heard. The pastor stepped to the pulpit to read the Scriptures, but not a sound was heard.

The congregation joined in repeating the prayer, but not a single sound was heard. The pastor again stepped to the pulpit, and went through all the motions of preaching, but the man with the angel heard nothing. So he turned to the angel and said,

"What does this mean? I see that a service is being held, but I hear nothing."

The angel replied, "You hear nothing because there is nothing to be heard. You see this service just as God sees it. These are not putting their hearts into it, and so God hears nothing. He hears only that which comes from the heart, and not that which comes from the lips only."

As the angel was speaking, back in the last pew they heard a child saying, "Our Father, which art in heaven, hallowed be thy name," etc. The angel said, "You are hearing the only part of this service that God hears. He hears this little child's prayer because she means what she says, and put her heart and soul in it."[57]

Can your praise be heard by God? Or are you talking to yourself?

---

[56] William R. White. *Stories for the Journey.* (Minneapolis, MN: Augsburg Publishing House, 1988), pp.63-64. Used by permission of Augsburg Fortress.

[57] Selected from *The Gospel for Youth.* Walter B. Knight. *Knight's Treasury of 2,000 Illustrations*, pp.447-448.

PRACTICAL ILLUSTRATIONS

10-237

PRAYER

1 Thessalonians 1:1-4

(POSB: Note 5)

Asking for God's Help

It has been said that God runs the world through those who pray. True as that is, many churches fail to pray as they should. Certainly, prayer is talked about in the pulpits and classrooms of the churches. But how many churches genuinely practice what is being preached and taught? Listen to this striking example of *why* we are to pray:

> "I felt so helpless, so powerless. I was watching my father die in the intensive care unit of the hospital and could not do a thing." This is the testimony of a man who had just prayed for his father to recover from a massive heart attack. As he prayed for his physical recovery, he also prayed for the spiritual condition of his father. With a weak voice, the father told his son that he was trusting Christ and would be in heaven if he were to die.
>
> As the son waited for a report on the progress of the emergency by-pass surgery, questions filled his heart: "Lord, I'm a man of faith. But right now, my faith is so weak. I'm so frustrated. I wish I could physically pick up my father and help carry him across the finish line." During this healthy exchange between a man and his heavenly Father, God spoke to his heart these words of comfort and encouragement: "The purpose of prayer is simply asking God to do what is impossible for you to do."
>
> How simple, but so profound. Somehow, we have come to think that we can do some of God's work without His help.
>
> Four hours later, the doctor reported that his father was going to recover and be stronger than ever. The son had nothing to do with that surgery. He could only wait and pray. And *that* is the secret: allowing God to do what only He can do.

10-238

PRAYER

2 Thessalonians 3:1-5

(POSB: Note 1, point 1)

Heating the Church with Prayer

Many churches have books about prayer in their library. Classes are taught and sermons are preached every week about why we should pray. But in the final analysis, do many take prayer seriously enough to pray?

> Five ministerial students were visiting in London on a hot Sunday in July. While they were waiting for the doors [of the church] to open, a man approached and asked, "Gentlemen, would you like to see the heating apparatus of the church?" They thought, "How queer he is to want to show us the heating system on a hot day in July!"
>
> Following him, they came to a door. He quietly opened it and whispered: "There, sirs, is our heating apparatus!" Some seven hundred intercessors were kneeling in prayer, seeking an outpouring of God's Spirit upon the service which was soon to

begin in the Tabernacle. That unknown guide was [Charles] Spurgeon [the great pastor of the pulpit] himself![58]

What is fueling the fire in your church's furnace—a powerless program or a praying people?

❧

10-239

PRAYER

1 Timothy 2:1-8

(*POSB: Note 2*)

Pray for Government Leaders

As true believers we are not told to put our *trust* in rulers; we are told to *pray* for them. Our trust is to be in the Lord. Politicians are not the answer to our problems. Jesus is the answer.

Men who feared God established the United States. They knew that any drift from trusting in Him would lead to ruin. The people came in droves from all parts of the world in order to worship God as they saw fit. Listen in on the conversation of one of the early unnamed pilgrims as he prayed to God:

> "Almighty God, You know how hard this new land is for us. At any moment the King of England could cut off his support and leave us to starve. Lord, work in his heart and move him to grant us favor. The freedom to worship You in this new land has been so rich. Touch the king's heart in a way that will forever secure our ability to worship You in openness. The memories of spiritual slavery to the Church of England and the persecution for resisting their wishes is still very fresh in my mind. Forever burn the memories on my heart so that I will never take for granted my freedoms. May You grace our governor with Your wisdom. Grant him courage to lead us down the right path and may Your compassion fill his heart."

Prayers like these proved to be the source of God's blessing of America. Prayer and peace go hand in hand. Are your prayers making an impact on your leaders, your nation?

❧

10-240

PRAYER

1 Timothy 2:1-8

(*POSB: Note 4*)

Pray Wherever You Are

Does God limit our prayers? Does God listen only to the prayers made within the confines of the church walls? Of course not! Tragically, many in our culture have been bullied into thinking that prayer is for the church only.

---

[58] John Walvoord. *The Thessalonian Epistles.* (Grand Rapids, MI: Zondervan Publishing House, 1973), p.146.

PRACTICAL ILLUSTRATIONS

During the first 170 years of American history, prayer was considered an appropriate thing to do before a ballgame, before school, or during a session of Congress when the need for God's guidance was felt. Previous presidents have often called upon the name of God during times of national crisis.

Prayer was never meant to be segregated but to be included in the everyday affairs of believers. On one particular day, a jury had been called together to consider the fate of a person accused of murder. The jury consisted of people from a variety of backgrounds. As it turned out, the foreman of the jury was a woman who loved Jesus Christ. At the urging of another Christian on the jury, she was asked to begin their deliberations in prayer, asking God for His wisdom. Even those who did not know Christ entered in as they had to make some critical decisions in the hours to come.

Though prepared for a long and drawn-out deliberation, the jury reached their unanimous decision of guilty in less than an hour. In that secular jury room, God came at their invitation and gave them exactly what they had asked for—His wisdom.

Are you free enough to pray everywhere?

10-241

PRAYER

2 Timothy 1:1-5

(POSB: Note 4)

Praying for Young Believers

Do your prayers for other believers really make a difference? The prayers of one man did in the life of a man we will call Ron.

Like most young men, Ron was seeking direction for his life. High school was passing all too quickly and now college was right around the corner. Years earlier in church Ron had made a commitment to Christ, but because no one had discipled him, he was stunted in his spiritual growth.

But Ron came to a fork in the road when he went on a spiritual retreat with his youth group. Should he follow through with his earlier commitment to Christ or listen to the call of the world? In God's perfect timing, God touched Ron's heart and lit a fire in his soul that burned into his adult life, then later into full-time service for the Lord.

Months after Ron's encounter with the Lord, he discovered that an elderly Christian man had been praying for him for years. "Mr. Jordan, what in the world compelled you to pray for me?" Mr. Jordan smiled and said, "Ron, His love for me compels me to pray for men like you. I do not know what God will make out of you, but I know that prayer moves His hand to work in a way that He can use you for His glory."

Are you praying for God to work in some young believer's life?

94

PRACTICAL ILLUSTRATIONS

10-242

PRAYER

Philemon 1-7

(POSB: Note 4)

Reaching Out to God

Every believer needs to pray. But do we really understand how to tap into the powerful resource of prayer?

> The little girl's eyes were wide open as she drank in the wonders of the popular vacation attraction called Disney World. The lights, the colors, the costumed characters, and the rides made quite an impression on the young child. But another attraction also captivated her attention. She could not stop talking about the bathroom sinks. Whenever she would hold her little hands over the sink, the water would automatically turn on. When she removed her hands from the sink, the water would automatically turn off. Unknown to her, an electronic sensor turned the water flow on and off. Marveling to her mother, the little girl exclaimed, "Mom. Now I know why they call it the Magic Kingdom!"

The simplest things are sometimes the most amazing. All we have to do is go to God in prayer, and the God of the Universe, the Creator of all mankind, hears and answers our prayers. God is not the One who cuts Himself off from us. He is constant; He is always there. It is when *we withdraw from Him* that the power is cut off, when the Spirit no longer guides and directs us. As long as we are standing in the right place, in Christ, with our hands reaching up to God, God will supply our every need.

◦◦◦

10-243

PRAYER

1 Timothy 2:1-8

(POSB: Note 1)

Recommitting to Prayer

One of the greatest challenges issued to believers is to pray. But do you pray like your prayers make a difference? For many years, Patrick thought prayer was a good idea; he even bought books on prayer. But prayer was not a *priority* to him. Ironically, Patrick had just been appointed chairman of his church's missions committee, which to him meant running the organization like a business...until he met Tim.

Tim was a missionary from China who was home on furlough after an emotionally and spiritually draining time on the mission field. Tim came to Patrick's first missions committee meeting in order to report on his ministry. Tim opened his report with these remarks:

> "Without the faithful prayers of this committee and its chairman, I would not be here today. Many times, my wife and I were on the verge of quitting, leaving China behind in the ruin of our failed attempts to share the gospel with those precious people. But just when we started to pack, we remembered all the folks back home who prom-

ised to pray for us. Patrick, I'd like to thank you and your committee for your faithfulness in prayer."

Patrick sunk in his seat as he mumbled, "You're welcome Tim. " Later, Patrick had this conversation with God: "Lord, I'm sorry for being so slack. If I had taken the time to pray for Tim and his wife, they would have been spared a lot of grief. I commit myself to a renewed prayer-life, with Your help."

On a sign in front of Patrick's church was this message: "Seven Days Without Prayer Makes One Weak." Your lack of prayer not only weakens your life, it affects others as well. Who needs your help today? Pray!

❧

10-244

PRAYER

1 Timothy 2:1-8　　　　　　　　　　**Satan Means Business**

(POSB: Introduction)

Would you pray any differently if you could actually see into the spiritual world, into the spiritual dimension of being? If that kind of sight could be granted for a moment, you would see the intense conflict being waged for your soul. You would quickly realize that Satan's fight for your soul is no game. Satan means business.

But know this: the Christian believer has been given a strategic part to play in waging war against Satan's onslaught against humanity. The prayers of intercession that are offered up to God are like destructive missiles to the enemy's plans. Are you doing your part?

❧

10-245

PRIDE

1 Timothy 6:3-5　　　　**What Goes Up Must Come Down**

(POSB: Note 2)

A false teacher thinks that he is God's gift to the world. Instead of true humility, his arrogant pride exposes his true motives—fame and glory. Al Bryant shares an example of a man who allowed pride to ruin his ministry.

One of [Charles] Spurgeon's students went into a pulpit with every expression of confidence, but he had an extremely difficult time. He came down distressed, almost brokenhearted, and he went to Spurgeon about it. The words of Spurgeon to him were these, "If you had gone up as you came down, you would have come down as you went up."[59]

The same thing that is true of physical gravity is true of spiritual pride: What goes up must come down.

❧

---

[59] Paul Lee Tan. *Encyclopedia of 7,700 Illustrations: Signs of the Times*, p.1100.

PRACTICAL ILLUSTRATIONS

10-246

PURITY

1 Thessalonians 4:1-8

(POSB, Notes 2, 3)

Drawing on Christ's Strength

Have you been trying to live a pure, moral life in your own strength? No man can succeed in this on his own. In order to walk in a way that will please God, you must ask Him for His power.

> Samuel Pearce...at the time of his conversion...resolved to formally dedicate himself to the Lord. He drew up a covenant; and, to make it more solemn and binding, he signed it with blood drawn from his own body.
> But afterwards, failing in his vows, he was plunged into great distress. Driven, therefore, into a more complete examination of his motives, he was led to see that he had been relying too much on his own strength; and, carrying the blood-signed covenant to the top of his father's house, he tore it into pieces and scattered it to the winds, and resolved...to depend upon the peace-making and peace-keeping blood of Christ.[60]

Any effort to be morally pure without God's help is ultimately doomed to failure. But when you draw upon God's strength, you have chosen the path of success.

❧

10-247

REBUKE

Titus 3:8-11

(POSB: Note 3)

How to Confront a Heretic

There is no worse perversion than knowingly twisting Scripture for one's own personal benefit. Here is one example of how it was done.

> Ben was a teacher who had mastered the art of abusing Scripture. His method for lesson preparation was simple: "Get my opinion on paper and then find a Bible verse that will back me up." As Ben taught, he would prove his opinion by showing how the Bible agreed with him.
> One day a class member confronted Ben and said, "Ben, how on earth did you come up with that one? Don't you know that you've got to keep each verse in its proper context? It is your responsibility to teach what the Bible says—not what you think it says about your opinion."

Confronting heretics is not an easy task, but God commands us to reject them, to take a stand against those who teach contrary to the Word of God.

❧

---

[60] Elon Foster, Editor. *6,000 Classic Sermon Illustrations*, p.61.

PRACTICAL ILLUSTRATIONS

10-248

REBUKE

Titus 1:10-16

(POSB: Note 2)

The Truth Sets People Free

Are you a little afraid of speaking the truth (the Word of God) to a false teacher or one of his followers? Just having the weapon of truth inside your heart will never intimidate a false teacher. As a believer, you must be aggressive and fight for the truth—not just to win the argument but to win the soul!

Steve had two goals in life: 1) get a good education; 2) get rich fast.

Steve directed his goal for education to the medical field. Over the course of time, he graduated at the head of his class and was soon practicing medicine in a large city. With goal number one completed, his next task was to cash in and make a lot of money. After doing some research, Steve chose to become a full-time abortionist. Being a product of his culture, his view of life was cheap. He saw his career as an economic opportunity not a moral issue. It did not take long for Steve to start making money. In fact, it seemed people were throwing their money at him for his services. Feeling very satisfied with his career choice, Steve began to settle down and enjoy life.

But his enjoyment was to be short-lived. After performing hundreds of abortions, Steve had a chance encounter with Mary, another doctor in the community who was also a believer. Mary was greatly respected and even loved throughout the community because she reached out to people and took time to minister to them. But when it came to Steve, she disagreed with his career choice. Yet Mary knew if God could change the man, the man would change his career. Her inclination was right. Mary invited Steve and his wife to her house to look at a video on childbirth. From conception to birth, the Christian perspective of life was shared. Steve became very sober. Light had pierced his darkened heart.

"Mary, thank you for showing me this. I had no idea there were real people in those wombs. Will God ever forgive me for what I've done?"

God did forgive Steve. Steve became a strong Christian believer and a strong voice for the innocent lives he had once taken. Why did Steve change? Because someone was willing to rebuke him, but in such a way that allowed the light of God's truth to come into his heart.

Today, the truth still sets people free. Use it!

10-249

RELATIONSHIPS

1 Timothy 5:1-2

(POSB: Note 2)

Bridging the Generation Gap

One of the greatest challenges in the field of human relationships is to cross over generational lines and relate to older or younger people. Here is one example of an older man who found a way to bridge the gap.

PRACTICAL ILLUSTRATIONS

Everyone knew him as Papa K. He was a very busy person, but he always had time for young people searching for the meaning to life. What made Papa K. so unique was his willingness to trust teenagers with ministry responsibilities. He trained kids to do everything from running a Christian coffeehouse to sharing their personal testimonies.

Not once did he compromise. The young people could count on his unconditional love. Because they knew he was genuine, the kids accepted Papa K.'s direction and even his constructive criticism. Once their mistakes or flaws were addressed, the young people would repent and then move on towards a greater maturity in their Christian journey. As a result of his personal touch, many young people went on to become faithful husbands and wives, loving fathers and mothers, hard-working and honest employees. And just as important, he taught them by example to get involved in the lives of other believers, discipling them just as he had done.

Sure, Papa K. took risks. Some kids failed to handle their responsibilities. But the fruit of his ministry affected thousands of lives.

Whether you are in the younger group or the older group, what can you do to bridge the generation gap?

10-250

RELATIONSHIPS

1 Timothy 5:1-2

(POSB: Introduction)

Treating Each Other as Family

A joke is told that asks this question: What do you get when an elephant sits on a fence? The answer is a broken fence. We can take some liberty with this joke and ask another question: What do you get when a Christian with a critical spirit "sits on" or attempts to correct another Christian? The answer is a broken relationship. Do not be mistaken: there is a duty to correct and discipline various age groups. But how?

The instructions are clear: the members of a church are to treat each other as family members. In no sense is any member to be rebuked. "Rebuke" means to be severely censured, angrily reprimanded, violently reproached. When a family church member needs to be corrected, there is to be no severity, anger, or violence involved; no contempt or disgust. A church member is to be corrected and disciplined through entreaty, that is, through exhortation and encouragement, through appeal and pleading.

Healthy relationships within the church are vital. When damaged, they hinder the work of the Holy Spirit. We must do all we can to restore fellowship with Christian brothers and sisters. Remember, restoration—not reproach—is the goal.

PRACTICAL ILLUSTRATIONS

10-251
RESPECT
1 Thessalonians 5:12-28   **Respect for Church Leaders**
(POSB: Note 1)

It is crucial to the life of a church that its leaders be respected. For where there is no respect, the ministry of the church implodes into spiritual ruin. Warren Wiersbe illustrates this point very well.

> According to Martin L. Gross in his book, *The Psychological Society*, more than 60,000 guidance workers and 7,000 school psychologists work in our American public education system; and many of them function as substitute parents. Many students need counseling, but no professional worker can take the place of a loving, faithful father or mother.
>
> When our oldest son entered high school, he met his assigned counselor. "Now, if you have any problems, feel free to come to me," the counselor said. Our son replied, "If I have any problems, I'll talk to my father!" He was not being disrespectful or unappreciative of the counselor, but he was giving expression of a basic principle: children need the leadership and guidance that only parents can give.
>
> God has ordained leadership for the local church. It is true that we are "all one in Christ Jesus" (Galatians 3:28); but it is also true that the Head of the church has given gifts to people, then given these people to the churches to exercise His will (Ephes. 4:7-16). Just as the flock needs a shepherd (1 Peter 5:1-5), so the [church] family needs a leader[s].[61]

If the leaders in your church are not respected, the sheep will seek out other shepherds.

∽

10-252
RESTITUTION
Philemon 8-21   **Making a Wrong Right**
(POSB: Note 3)

When Jesus Christ touches someone's life, change is always evident. This change works itself into every area of life—especially in the area of integrity and wanting to make right previous mistakes.

> Larry was a rebel during his high school days. Heavy into the drug culture, he supported his habit by stealing and selling the stolen goods to a pawn shop. One day Jesus Christ intervened and dramatically changed his hard heart. Larry cleaned himself up. The drugs were flushed down the toilet. A love for God and His Word filled the void that drugs had failed to supply. Larry became a vocal witness to his former drug friends.
>
> As Larry continued to grow in Christ, he became convicted about righting the wrongs of his previous lifestyle. He went from store to store speaking with managers about what he had stolen in years past, apologizing for his actions and offering to work

---

[61] Warren W. Wiersbe. *The Bible Exposition Commentary*, Vol.2. (Wheaton, IL: Victor Books, 1989), p.186-187.

out a plan of restitution. The response of one manager sums the reaction of most: "Why did you come back? You had already gotten away with this and no one knew" the manager said.

"Sir, I came back because Jesus Christ saved me. I'm living for Him now and He doesn't want a petty thief serving Him."

The story does not end here. Larry's witness went on to affect many in the community, including his drug friends and others whom he had wronged in the past.

When Jesus Christ saves you, the change should be complete. God wants people to have a right relationship with Him and with each other.

10-253

RESTORATION

Philemon 22-25

(POSB: Note 3)

Giving a Second Chance

The church has been noted by some to be the only army that shoots its wounded, that is, that turns its back on those who have fallen in sin. There is no question; this world is a battlefield pitting believers against unbelievers every day. Like it or not, casualties are to be expected when an army is at war. Believers are frequently wounded by their involvement in the conflict. But God has made a way for the wounded to recover, to be restored back to spiritual health once again.

Years ago a noted spiritual leader of a large parachurch organization fell into sexual immorality. While others might have strongly denied any wrongdoing, this leader was heart-broken that he had betrayed his wife. Before his sin was exposed for all the world to see, he asked for forgiveness from his wife, his organization, and his church. He was a genuinely repentant man.

The elders of his church were very compassionate people. They saw in this man a unique gift that God had given to the Body of Christ. It was a gift too valuable to dispose of. The elders made it their purpose to restore the man back to spiritual health. For nearly two years, they covered their brother with love. They set up a program of restoration that helped heal the wounds in his marriage. This program also helped him put protective habits in place that prevented the sexual sin from rearing its ugly head again.

Does God restore? Yes—He forgives and restores if a person is truly repentant. If God gives second chances—can you do any less?

PRACTICAL ILLUSTRATIONS

10-254

RESTORATION

2 Timothy 2:22-26

(POSB: Note 4)

Rescuing Through Love

It was American president Teddy Roosevelt who made famous the quote, "Speak softly and carry a big stick; you will go far." His point was to show meekness, but to be able to back it up if needed.

> Dennis was a building contractor with a knack for causing division. With some degree of satisfaction, he reveled in causing friction among co-workers. It did not take long for his reputation to precede him in business dealings, and many people in the community avoided him.
>
> Pete, on the other hand, was a local banker who saw Dennis as a personal challenge. While others avoided Dennis, Pete felt the Lord leading him to reach out to the abrasive man with the gospel. A man of strong integrity and meekness, Pete had a certain way about him. He befriended and loved the unlovable—unconditionally. Pete's approach caught Dennis by surprise.
>
> As a result of Pete's patience and meekness over many months, Dennis saw his need for Christ and repented of his sins. Dennis was pulled from the lethal snare of the devil to the lasting salvation of the Lord.

Who do you know who needs the Lord? Neither argument, criticism, nor condemnation will win them. But gentle correction will show Christ's willingness to seek and to save.

10-255

RESURRECTION

1 Thessalonians 4:13-5:3

(POSB: Note 1)

The Blessed Hope of the Resurrection

One of the great hopes of the Christian believer is the hope of the resurrection.

> Once a party of sailors on shore on [an] island of the sea ate freely of [a] plant that threw them into a deep sleep. As they returned not, others came in search of their companions and found them lying apparently dead.
>
> Anxiously they set to work to rouse the drugged sleepers, and the recovery of the first was a glad omen that the rest...would revive, as in time they did.[62]

You have no need to worry about the fate of those saints who have fallen asleep in Christ. They will rise again!

---

[62] Elon Foster, Editor. *6,000 Classic Sermon Illustrations*, p.670.

PRACTICAL ILLUSTRATIONS

10-256

RETURN OF CHRIST

1 Thessalonians 4:13-5:3

(POSB: Note 3, point 1)

The Great Reunion

Believer's can take great comfort knowing that departed loved ones (in Christ) will be seen again. There is comfort and solace in the Lord and in His plan.

> In *Love and Duty* Anne Purcell writes about seeing Major Jim Statler standing with her pastor outside his study after a Sunday service. She knew instantly that he was there with news about her husband Ben on active duty in Viet Nam. As she feared, Jim gave her a chilling message: "He was on a helicopter that was shot down ...he's missing in action."
>
> Anne recalls, "Somewhere in the back of my mind, a little candle flame flickered. This tiny flame was the vestige of my faith." Days passed without word. To her, being an MIA wife was like being in limbo. She found herself only able to pray one thing: "Help me, dear Father." She says, "I hung onto this important truth—that He would help me—and the flickering flame of my candle of faith began to grow." Then, one day, she noticed a white dove sitting in her yard. It was particularly beautiful, very still and quiet, and a highly uncommon sight in her neighborhood. She took it as a sign from God that He was, indeed, always near.
>
> For five years, Anne Purcell clung to the fact that God was near. Little did she know that during those years before she was reunited with her husband, he was whispering to her from a POW cell, "Anne, find solace and strength in the Lord."[63]

What a great reunion there will be at the coming of the Lord! Believers, have faith in this promise of comfort from God. Remember, sorrow looks back. Worry looks around. But faith looks up.

෴

10-257

RETURN OF CHRIST

1 Thessalonians 4:13-5:3

(POSB: Introduction)

The Groom Is Coming

Ever since Christ left the earth and ascended into heaven, the church has been waiting for His return. Just as a bride anxiously awaits the call to march down the aisle, believers await the glorious day when Christ will call for them.

That wedding day is coming soon. Will you be ready to march when the cue comes? No one can afford to be late for this wedding of all ages. Do not become weary in your waiting: the Groom is coming for you.

෴

---

[63] *God's Little Devotional Book.* (Tulsa, OK: Honor Books, 1995), pp. 80-81.

PRACTICAL ILLUSTRATIONS

10-258

RETURN OF CHRIST

1 Thessalonians 5:4-11

(POSB: Introduction)

The Most Phenomenal Event of All

There is a particular circus that advertises itself as the greatest show on earth. Amazing feats of skill and daring are featured in this three-ring circus. At the end of the breath-taking show people leave, shaking their heads over all they have witnessed. Great as the performance is, the Christian believer knows that an even more spectacular event is on the way, one that will make all of man's great shows pale in comparison.

The return of Jesus Christ is to be the most phenomenal event in all of human history. It will be the most amazing event ever to be witnessed by the eyes of man. Its importance cannot be overstressed, for when Christ returns, both the blessing and the judgment of God will fall upon the earth. Genuine believers will be blessed and unbelievers will suffer the terrifying wrath of God.

10-259

RETURN OF CHRIST

1 Thessalonians 5:4-11

(POSB: Note 2)

Preparing for Christ's Return

Do you stay focused on the things of the Lord? Will you be ready if He comes today?

Lord Shackleton once went to search for the South Pole. He had to turn back, leaving some of his men on Elephant Island amid the ice and snow. He promised to come back for them. He finally reached South Georgia, where he secured another ship and supplies; and then went back to get his men.

He tried to reach Elephant Island, but failed time after time. Suddenly one day there appeared an open place through the ice leading to the island! Quickly he ran his men through the open place, got his men on board the ship, and came out again, just before the ice crashed together. It was done in half an hour.

When the excitement was partly over, he asked one of the men who had been on the island, "How did it happen that you were all packed and ready for my coming? You were standing on the shore ready to leave at a moment's notice."

The man replied, "Sir, you said that you would come back for us, and we never gave up hope. Whenever the sea was partly clear of ice, we rolled up our sleeping bags and packed our things, saying, "Maybe Shackleton will come today." We were always ready for your coming."[64]

Jesus will come suddenly. This could be the day. Are you ready to go at a moment's notice?

10-260

RETURN OF CHRIST

Titus 2:11-15

(POSB: Note 3)

Watching for Christ's Return

How eager are you for the return of Christ? Is it just a passing thought or are you searching like this little child?

Mary idolized her older brother Johnny. He always took time to make her feel special. But she was only five years old and Johnny was twenty. One day Johnny put her on his lap and said, "Mary, I've got to go and work at a job that is a long way from home. I'll be gone for a long time, but I promise I'll come home again. One day I'll walk right down the sidewalk, and as soon as I see you, I'll run to grab hold of you. Don't forget to watch for me."

After a good cry they hugged, and then Johnny turned and walked away. Mary peered with her face to the window until he disappeared. As the months went by, she regularly pressed her face to the window, straining to look for her brother. Some of her family said: "Johnny won't come back for a long, long time. Why don't you go play and have some fun?" "Because he promised me he would come back," Mary would say with all the conviction a five year old could produce.

Through the weeks and months, Mary faithfully kept her eyes open, looking for the return of her dear brother. And then it happened one day just like he said. As she stared through the window, a tiny speck caught her attention. As the speck grew larger, she could see it was Johnny! He was not walking; he was running. Johnny wanted to see Mary as much as she wanted to see him. After grabbing her in his arms he asked, "Have you been watching for me like I asked you to?"

It is the responsibility of every believer to watch diligently for Christ's return. What will be *your* answer when He asks: "Have you been watching for My return as I asked you to?"

---

[64] *Gospel Herald.* Walter B. Knight. *3,000 Illustrations for Christian Service*, p.605.

10-261

RIGHTEOUSNESS

2 Timothy 4:6-8

(POSB: Note 3, point 2)

Man's Motivation: A Crown or Applause?

Think about this for a moment: What motivates you on your journey to heaven? For some, the answer is blunt—they do not want to go to hell. The apostle Paul had a far more mature reason for wanting to go to heaven. He knew that the Lord Jesus Christ would be there waiting for him. And when he got to heaven, he knew that he would be accepted by God—an acceptance not based upon his performance but upon Christ's great sacrifice on the cross.

A young man, having studied violin under a great master, was giving his first recital. Following each number, despite the cheers of the crowd, the boy seemed dissatisfied. Even after the last number, with the shouts louder than ever, the boy stood watching an old man in the top balcony. Finally the old man smiled and nodded approval. Immediately the young man relaxed and beamed his happiness. The plaudits [praise] of the crowd meant nothing until he had won the approval of the master.[65]

If you are a believer in Jesus Christ, you have a crown awaiting you in heaven—your eternal reward for service. The temporary applause of men will never satisfy you like the eternal approval of God.

ॐ

10-262

SACRIFICE

Titus 3:12-15

(POSB: Note 1)

Sacrifice for a Cause

A believer's level of commitment is directly related to his willingness to sacrifice for the cause of Christ. Listen to this amazing account:

Robert Chesebrough believed in his product. He's the fellow who invented Vaseline, a petroleum jelly refined from rod wax, the ooze that forms on shafts of oilrigs. He so believed in the healing properties of his product that he became his own guinea pig. He burned himself with acid and flame; he cut and scratched himself so often and so deeply that he bore the scars of his tests the rest of his life. But he proved his product worked. People had only to look at his wounds, now healed, to see the value of his work—and the extent of his belief.[66]

Is your commitment to Christ real? Real enough to sacrifice and suffer—for Him, for others? To do whatever God wants you to do, when He wants you to do it, wherever He wants you to go?

ॐ

---

65 Walter B. Knight. *Knight's Master Book of 4,000 Illustrations*, pp. 571-572.

66 Craig B. Larson. *Illustrations for Preaching & Teaching*, p. 14.

10-263

SALVATION

2 Thessalonians 2:13-17   **Do Not Be Left Behind**

(POSB: Note 1)

As American involvement in the Vietnam War came to an end, the city of Saigon was the last line of a faltering defense. In the final hours before Saigon fell into the hands of the enemy, panic was rampant throughout the city—especially at the American Embassy and the airport.

Vietnamese who had been loyal to the Americans were scampering for some way to escape the country. They knew if they remained they would be in grave danger. As the aggressive enemy troops continued to push into the city, the anxiety level intensified. Soon, there were no more flights leaving the airport.

According to official reports, there was a throng of people left after the last plane was out of harm's way. Those who had caught the last flight out had made sure their affairs were in order. Their paperwork was current and their tickets reserved a place for them. For those who were left behind, all hope was lost. The last plane out was gone—without them.

Will you be on the last plane out? Or because of your rejection of Christ, will you be left behind when He returns for His own?

෯

10-264

SALVATION

Titus 3:3   **Life Without God**

(POSB: Introduction)

What do you look like first thing in the morning? If you are like most people, you probably look pretty rough. As you stare into the bathroom mirror (if you dare), you see your hair disheveled, maybe even dirty. Your eyes may be puffy or bloodshot. Your face lacks color and energy. In short, before you meet the public, your mission is to change what you see into what you want to be seen.

Similarly, before Christ came into our lives, we looked pretty rough. We were living lives apart from Christ, not necessarily involved in gross sin, but certainly guilty of sin. And being guilty, we stand imperfect before God and short of His glory. Therefore, we all need to be saved through the Lord Jesus Christ. We need Him to come into our lives and to take away our sin and its ugly effects.

෯

10-265

SALVATION

Titus 3:4-7   **Mercy: Not Getting What We Deserve**

(POSB: Note 1, point 4)

It has been said that grace is getting what we do *not* deserve and mercy is not getting what we *do* deserve. Because we are sinners, we deserve to face the full force of the law—hell, separation from God, spiritual death

PRACTICAL ILLUSTRATIONS

for eternity. But God chose instead to be merciful to man, to give him the opportunity to be saved. Such is the case in the following account.

> Quite a few years ago, Governor Neff of the State of Texas received an invitation to speak at one of the penitentiaries in that state. He spoke to the assembled prisoners, and afterward said that he would be around for a while to listen to anything any of the convicts might wish to tell him. He would take as much time as they wanted, and anything they would tell him would be kept in confidence.
>
> The convicts began to come, one at a time. One after another told him a story of how they had been unjustly sentenced, were innocent, and wished to get out. Finally one man came through who said to him, "Governor Neff, I do not want to take much of your time. I only want to say that I really did what they convicted me of . But I have been here a number of years. I believe I have paid my debt to society, and that, if I were to be released, I would be able to live an upright life and show myself worthy of your mercy."
>
> This was the man whom Governor Neff pardoned.[67]

This man was guilty; he deserved to be punished. But he acknowledged his crime, humbled himself, and asked forgiveness of the governor. That is exactly what sinful man must do with the Almighty God. He knows our sin. We deserve His wrath and punishment. But if we will confess our sin, humble ourselves, and ask for forgiveness, God will be merciful and offer us salvation!

> "For God so loved the world, that he gave his only begotten Son, that whosoever believeth in him should not perish, but have everlasting life" (John 3:16).

10-266

SALVATION

Titus 3:4-7

(POSB: Introduction)

The Miraculous Power of God

Think for a moment. When do you most feel the need for a miracle in your life? Is it...

- when you are sick and no help seems available?
- when you are going through some personal crisis?
- when you are facing financial disaster?
- when you are out of work and in need of a job?
- when you have lost a loved one and can't handle the grief?
- when you feel overwhelmed because of circumstances?

No matter who you are or where you live, the miracle-working power of God is at work in some way. Have you ever experienced His healing power? Have your material needs ever been met in a miraculous way? Have you ever seen His protection over your life? Through every

---

[67] Ted Kyle and John Todd, Compilers. *A Treasury of Bible Illustrations.* (Chattanooga, TN: AMG Publishers, 1995), p.288.

generation, God has proven faithful in meeting the needs of His children. But God has done so much more than just work miracles in the physical realm. The greatest miracle of all was when He sent His Son, the Lord Jesus Christ, to save us from our sins.

The salvation of your soul is the most miraculous thing that can ever happen. If God can do something this glorious, can you trust Him to do the *less difficult* things that come your way in life?

❦

10-267

SALVATION

1 Timothy 1:12-17

Run to the Savior

(POSB: Note 2)

Scripture is very clear about who has taken the initiative to save us. Unquestionably, it is Jesus Christ. Unfortunately, we often run away from the only One who can save us!

In 1981, a Minnesota radio station reported a story about a stolen car in California. Police were staging an intense search for the vehicle and the driver, even to the point of placing announcements on local radio stations to contact the thief.

On the front seat of the stolen car sat a box of crackers that, unknown to the thief, were laced with poison. The car owner had intended to use the crackers as rat bait. Now the police and the owner of the VW Bug were more interested in apprehending the thief to save his life than to recover the car.

So often when we run from God, we feel it is to escape his punishment. But what we are actually doing is eluding his rescue.[68]

Are you running from God's punishment or from His rescue?

❦

10-268

SALVATION

Titus 3:4-7

The Worthless Currency of the World

(POSB: Note 3, point 2)

Have you trusted Jesus Christ to forgive your sins? Imagine, if you will, that you are on location at "Heaven's Savings & Loan."

Several businessmen and women are at the bank to turn in their worthless "currency." One by one, each person has come to realize that his trust in currency has been misplaced. And now each one, without exception, is bankrupt.

The Banker has scheduled an interview with each professional. Sitting in a chair across from his desk, the Banker asks Jim, "What did you place your trust in?" With his head bowed low, Jim replied, "In my family connections. My grandparents were active church-goers." The Banker gave Jim an envelope and said, "This will take care of you."

---

[68] Craig B. Larson, Editor. *Illustrations for Preaching & Teaching*, p.207.

PRACTICAL ILLUSTRATIONS

Mary was the next person to meet with the Banker. "Mary, what did you place your trust in?" "In my education. I spent a lot of money to get the best education money could buy." Even as she spoke these words, a gnawing feeling came over her. It was a feeling of great emptiness. As he did with Jim, the Banker gave Mary an envelope and assured her, "This will take care of you."

One by one they came—each without the means to live. When they opened their envelopes, each saw a blood-stained nail with these instructions included:

> Take this nail and that which you trust
> And exchange them both for life, you must
> I have paid the price that you might live
> Your trust in Me is what you must give

We are no different than these individuals. Every one of us was spiritually bankrupt. Thankfully, Jesus Christ saw our desperate condition and chose to help us. Our righteousness can never buy salvation. No, it takes something much more powerful and something lasting. It takes a loving God who gave His Son to die for us. And it takes our believing that God's Son did die for us, that He justifies us, counts us righteous. Have you made your appointment with the Heavenly Banker to exchange your worthless currency?

10-269

SANCTIFICATION

1 Thessalonians 4:1-8   **This Poisonous Culture**

(POSB: Note 2, point 3)

What is called "popular" in your culture is not always the best option for the believer.

A man living in a forested area found his home overrun with mice—too many to exterminate with traps. So he bought a few boxes...[of poison] and distributed them around the house, including one under his bed. That night he couldn't believe his ears; below him was a feeding frenzy.

In the morning he checked the box and found it licked clean. Just to make sure the plan worked, he bought and placed another box. Again, the mice went for the flavored poison like piranha.

But the tasty and popular nighttime snack did its deadly work. In the days that followed, all was quiet. Just because something is popular doesn't mean it's good for you. In fact, it can be deadly—like sin.[69]

---

[69] Craig B. Larson, Editor. *Illustrations for Preaching & Teaching*, p.227.

PRACTICAL ILLUSTRATIONS

10-270

SERVICE

2 Timothy 2:14-21

(POSB: Note 4, point 2)

How to Be Holy

Real holiness comes from departing from iniquity, from turning our backs on sin and leaving it behind. It will not happen all by itself. As D. A. Carson noted:

> People do not drift toward holiness. Apart from grace-driven effort, people do not gravitate toward godliness, prayer, obedience to Scripture, faith, and delight in the Lord.
>
> We drift toward compromise and call it tolerance; we drift toward disobedience and call it freedom; we drift toward superstition and call it faith. We cherish the indiscipline of lost self-control and call it relaxation; we slouch toward prayerlessness and delude ourselves into thinking we have escaped legalism; we slide toward godlessness and convince ourselves we have been liberated.[70]

10-271

SERVICE

1 Timothy 4:6-16

(POSB: Note 12)

On Guard Against Worldliness

We seldom take the time to look in the mirror to examine our lives. While caring for others is important, taking car of ourselves is just as essential. Remember that a part of the greatest commandment is to love your neighbor as you love yourself.

> Jim, a young Christian businessman, planned for success and was pretty close to fulfilling his desire before he turned 30. During his quest, sleep did not matter. Eating right did not matter. Physical exercise was only an inconvenience. God, church, prayer, and personal Bible study did not matter. But in his "busyness," he almost lost his grip on life.
>
> Subtle things began to crop up in Jim's life: depression took the place of joy...slackness replaced discipline...a sharp, critical tongue quenched his normally friendly personality. Jim's thought-life began to wander...his job performance began to slip and to draw his employer's attention.
>
> Staring into the bathroom mirror, he examined the pathetic figure in the reflection. His marriage was on the rocks and his love for God was lukewarm at best. "Where did I go wrong?" he asked himself. The truth is that Jim had been more concerned about success than about anything or anyone else on earth. He had become enslaved by the passion to succeed at any cost. The result: he was on the brink of destroying his life and ripping his family apart.
>
> But Jim was fortunate. Some Christian friends rallied around to help restore him both physically and spiritually. From the ashes of his brokenness evolved a man who

---

[70] D. A. Carson. Quoted in *Reflections. Christianity Today* (7-31-00).

PRACTICAL ILLUSTRATIONS

was better able and more willing to serve the Lord and to care for his family and him-self.

Are you guarding your physical fitness, your spiritual fitness, and re-maining true to God's Word in your lifestyle? Remember that you cannot effectively influence others for Christ if you do not first take care of your-self.

10-272
SERVICE
2 Timothy 1:1-5   **Setting Priorities**
(POSB: Introduction)

Think for a moment: What are your priorities in life? What brings you joy?
- recreation?
- material possessions?
- position?
- power?
- sex?
- authority?
- family?
- church?
- helping others?

There are two kinds of Christians believers:
- those whose lives have purpose and inner fulfillment
- those whose lives do not

The world says...
- hoard your resources
- look out for #1 (yourself)
- think only of yourself and your own needs

New Testament Christianity is radically different. God has called each believer to a life of service, to a life of sacrifice. The believer is to...
- share what God has given
- deny self
- seek out those who are in need and minister to them

Now think about it again. As a Christian believer, are you making a positive impact for Christ? Will your current priorities make a significant difference in the big picture of life? Or are you just indifferent? God has given every believer the great privilege of serving Him, of living a life that really matters. Are you living life for the here and now or serving in light of eternity?

PRACTICAL ILLUSTRATIONS

10-273

SIN

1 Timothy 6:11-16   **What Is Sin?**

(POSB: Note 4)

Sometimes we treat God's commandments as options on a menu instead of as orders or instructions. But a failure to keep God's commandments is sin. What is sin? *Moody Monthly* makes this contribution:

- "Man calls it an accident; God calls it an abomination.
- "Man calls it a blunder; God calls it a blindness.
- "Man calls it a defect; God calls it a disease.
- "Man calls it chance; God calls it a choice.
- "Man calls it an error; God calls it an enmity
- "Man calls it a fascination; God calls it a fatality.
- "Man calls it an infirmity; God calls it an iniquity.
- "Man calls it a luxury; God calls it a leprosy.
- "Man calls it a liberty; God calls it lawlessness.
- "Man calls it a trifle; God calls it a tragedy.
- "Man calls it a mistake; God calls it a madness.
- "Man calls it a weakness; God calls it willfulness."[71]

What do you call a failure to keep God's commandments?

❧

10-274

SPIRITUAL STRENGTH

2 Thessalonians 1:1-5   **Being in Good Spiritual Shape**

(POSB: Introduction)

You have probably heard the phrase "No pain, no gain." If you want to strengthen your body, there is a certain amount of suffering that figures into the equation. In order to get into shape, you cannot just rest on the sofa and stare at an exercise video. You must decide what is important to you and then ask yourself this question: "Is the gain worth the pain?"

You can tell the importance of being in shape every time you climb several flights of stairs or run at break-neck speed in order to catch your connecting flight at the airport. If you are not in shape, you wheeze and hold your side in pain; if you are in shape you are comfortable and take it all in stride. Your choice to endure exercise, to endure the stress on your body, paid off when your body was called upon to perform.

The same is true with a church: a church is either strong or weak. And never is a church's spiritual strength more evident than when under savage attack or persecution. At such times believers must stand fast, be faithful, growing in the grace and peace of God.

❧

---

[71] *Moody Monthly.* Walter B. Knight. *Knight's Treasury of 2,000 Illustrations*, p.363.

PRACTICAL ILLUSTRATIONS

10-275

TEACHING

Titus 2:1-10

(POSB: Note 1)

Teaching for Change

Strange as it may seem, not every Sunday school class is taught by a strong or genuine believer. A striking example of one church follows:

> Otis had one of the biggest Sunday School classes, drawing a wide variety of people. There was standing room only in his class. Why did the people come? A lot of it had to do with his personality. He was a very friendly and charming man who knew how to mix in humor at the right time. Otis was a master of the punch line. His topics for discussion came right out of the weekly newspaper. His current events format was considered by many to be more relevant than a book that was more than 2,000 years old (the Bible).
>
> At the other end of the spectrum, Marsha's class was the only true Bible session offered by the church. When her class began, the numbers were small but the people had a deep hunger to study the Bible. Instead of just hearing Otis' opinions, they wanted to know God's opinion.
>
> Over the course of time and because of Marsha's faithfulness to teach even a few, the class outgrew its space and had to move to a bigger room. In the final analysis, a lot of people went *through* Otis' class. But few people were changed, really changed for Christ. Real change, eternal change, took place in Marsha's class. The lost were saved and believers grew in faith. The reason? Marsha's lessons came from the Book of Life—a Book whose words never change and always ring true!

10-276

TEMPTATION

1 Timothy 3:8-13

(POSB: Note 1, point 4)

Killing the Source of Sin

Talking about living a committed life is one thing, but actually *living it* is quite another.

> An old deacon who used to pray every Wednesday night at prayer meeting always concluded his prayer the same way: "And, Lord, clean all the cobwebs out of my life."
>
> The cobwebs were those things that ought not to have been there, but had gathered during the week. It got too much for one fellow in the prayer meeting, and he heard the old deacon one time too often. So when the man made that prayer, the fellow jumped to his feet and shouted: "Lord, Lord, don't do it! [Don't just clean the cobwebs.] Kill the spider!"[72]

That's good advice for every believer: Go to the source of your sin and kill the spider.

---

[72] Selected from *Gospel Herald*. Paul Lee Tan. *Encyclopedia of 7,700 Illustrations: Signs of the Times*, p.1234.

PRACTICAL ILLUSTRATIONS

10-277

TEMPTATION

1 Thessalonians 4:1-8

(POSB: Introduction)

The Painful Reality of Sin

Have you ever muttered these words: "If only I could take back what I have done"? A man named John said the same thing. Even though he had a beautiful wife and two precious children, he risked it all for a fleeting affair with another woman. During the time of this illicit relationship, he found creative ways to justify his behavior. But after his sin was exposed, his fragile world exploded into a million pieces.

His faithful wife was crushed. The two children cried over their fallen hero. John wished that he could die. He was truly sorry for his sin against God and against his family.

Normally during these kinds of earthquakes there are no survivors. But this family was fortunate. Through marriage counseling and the support of their church family, John's family was glued back together again. They were able to overcome this moral earthquake and to begin rebuilding their lives. Remember: no matter how attractive the sin, it is never worth the cost.

❧

10-278

TEMPTATION

1 Thessalonians 4:1-8

(POSB: Note 1, point 2, c)

Staying on Guard

Do not let down your guard. Never fool yourself into thinking you are above temptation or immoral behavior. Sin can invade your life and it will make every brazen attempt to do so.

Years ago, a German teenager flew an airplane from Germany to the heart of Moscow, Russia. He was able to fly completely unnoticed through the finest radar technology that money could buy. He landed his plane on the historic Red Square in Moscow, all to the amazement of the world and to the embarrassment of the Russian military.

There is a lesson in this event: *DO NOT LET DOWN YOUR GUARD*—not even for a moment. Keep a watchful eye out for incoming hostile temptation. The German teenager was harmless. But slackness can lull you into a deadly situation. Temptation may confront you today. Be ready. Stay on your guard.

❧

10-279

TRUST

Titus 1:5-9

(POSB: Introduction)

A Trustworthy Spiritual Leader

Of all the people who serve as leaders in your community, whom do you trust the most? Do you trust...

- your doctor?
- your banker?
- your pharmacist?

- your pastor?
- your mayor?
- your church elders?

All of these professions involve a great deal of responsibility, and they also require a great deal of trust on your part. When a person gets sick and needs care, trust is given to the doctor and pharmacist. When a community needs political leadership, trust is given at the ballot box to elect the person we feel will do the best job. When we deposit our hard-earned money in the bank, we trust the banker to take good care of what we give him. Without trust, life is difficult—if not impossible—to live. This is true in secular things. But trust is especially critical in our spiritual lives. This is the reason God holds the leaders of the church to such strict standards, standards that require a life of trustworthiness. Should lay believers be any *less* accountable for trustworthiness than their spiritual leaders? No, for we are all servants, ministers of God.

10-280

TRUTH

2 Timothy 4:1-5   **Does Your Life Reflect the Truth?**

(POSB: Note 3, point 1)

There are few things worse than mixing a little truth with a lot of error. In many congregations, compromise has replaced Biblical conviction. It was the great preacher Harry Ironside who illustrated the case well:

> A brilliant [liberal]...preacher...was bidding farewell to his congregation as he was about to leave them for a new parish.
> One of his young men approached him, and said: "Pastor, I am sorry we are losing you. Before you came I was one who did not care for God, man, or the Devil, but through your delightful sermons, I have learned to love them all!"[73]

Every believer's life is a sermon. What kind of message are you sharing with the world?

10-281

UNITY

1 Thessalonians 3:11-13   **A By-product of Love**

(POSB: Note 2, point 2)

It is the love of God that binds us together. In a body of believers unified by love, every believer has a very special part to play in building up the church.

> Dr. Halbeck, a missionary of the Church of England in the South of Africa, from the top of a neighboring hill saw lepers at work. He noticed two particularly, sowing peas

---

[73] Walter B. Knight. *Knight's Master Book of 4,000 Illustrations*, p. 503.

in the field. One had no hands; the other no feet—these members being wasted away by disease. The one who wanted the hands was carrying the other, who wanted the feet, upon his back; and he again carried the bag of seed, and dropped a pea every now and then, which the other pressed into the ground with his feet: and so they managed the work of one man between the two.

Such should be the true union of the members of Christ's body, in which all the members should have the same care one for another.[74]

The love of God will produce unity—people working as one. Are you working as an individual or as part of a team?

10-282

VICTORY

1 Thessalonians 2:13-20
(POSB: Introduction)

Strength to Win the Battle

Has a bully ever picked on you? Years ago, a popular advertisement was featured in a variety of magazines. Pictured was a 98-pound weakling lying on a beach brushing sand out of his face. How did the sand get there? A bully kicked it in his face. The intent of the advertisement was to touch the emotions of people who were fed up with getting picked on or stepped on by some bully in their lives. All a person had to do was fill out the coupon, enclose a personal check, and wait for the "anti-bully" kit. With newfound strength and a vision of being able to kick sand back in the face of the bully, a person would supposedly never fear the bully again.

In many ways, believers can relate to that 98-pound weakling. When it comes to confronting Satan and all the threatening problems of life, we often find ourselves flat on our backs, sand in our faces, waving the white flag of surrender. Instead of living like victorious Christians, we forfeit the battle without a fight. But if we want to be strong Christians, we must draw on God's strength not our own, and certainly not on anything the world has to offer.

A strong church is made up of strong believers, people who have trusted Jesus Christ as their Savior and Lord and who are continuing steadfast in Him.

10-283

WIDOWS

1 Timothy 5:3-16
(POSB: Note 5)

Caring for Widows

When adult children face the challenge of caring for a widowed parent, it does not have to be a one-way street. Granny is a good example.

---

[74] Elon Foster, Editor. *6,000 Sermon Illustrations*, p.428.

PRACTICAL ILLUSTRATIONS

Granny was Mary's mother. Mary's father had died years earlier and until recently her mother was doing just fine on her own. But with advancing age, she either had to move her mother to a retirement home or move her into her own home with herself and her family. It was obvious to Mary and her husband Dan that Granny needed to be brought into their home and be made a part of their family.

Having Granny in the home gave the grandchildren memories they would never forget. Did she put a strain on the family? Sure. But the blessings from having Granny live with them far outweighed any sacrifice that was made by Mary and Dan.

When Granny finally went home to be with the Lord, she did not leave an empty room behind. Instead, she left an abundance of great memories in the hearts of Mary's family.

Who can you reach out to today and touch with God's love?

10-284

WIDOWS

1 Timothy 5:3-16

(POSB: Note 1)

Demonstrating Your Christianity

Many people are indifferent to caring for the Christian widow. But look at how one particular church takes a practical and Biblical approach.

As Jane buried her precious husband, the crushing reality of his absence began to overwhelm her. During the forty-five years of their marriage, Sam paid the bills, balanced the checkbook, kept the cars running, and maintained their home with his "handy-man" talents. Now, all of his contributions were gone. "What on earth will I do?" Jane tossed this question back and forth against the walls of her broken heart.

What Jane did not know, but would soon come to realize, is that her church family was aware of her needs. They were committed to care for their widows. Bob was a professional auto mechanic who pledged to keep her car in running condition. Larry's position as a banker would prove to be an answer to Jane's prayers. He took responsibility for her financial affairs. The men's fellowship included her home in their out-reach as they took care of her household repairs and yard care.

None of this care escaped the attention of her younger sister Linda. Linda was also a widow but was not a Christian and had always mocked Jane for her naiveté. But because of the quality care these Christians gave her sister, Linda's closed heart began to open up and she eventually received Christ as her Savior. All because Christians cared.

How does your church care for widows?

PRACTICAL ILLUSTRATIONS

10-285

WIDOWS

1 Timothy 5:3-16   ## Support for Those in Need

(POSB: Introduction)

Do you know someone who has recently been widowed? How is that person doing? Do you even know?

> It took only a split second for Linda to lose her husband and become the sole surviving parent for their two young children. The grief and open-ended questions were very much a part of her devastated world. But even though the pain was great, she experienced an even greater sense of comfort as her church rallied to her side.
>
> The Christian believer is not exempt from the pain of a loved one's death. But there is a major difference. The believer has a valuable membership in the body of Christ, a group of people who have been given specific instructions on how to treat those who are hurting.

If you are hurting, do not withdraw into your pain. God has someone in mind who is ready to reach out to help you. But if you see someone else hurting, be alert. Maybe God has *you* in mind to do the reaching out.

෴

10-286

WILL OF GOD

Titus 1:1-4   ## The Desire for Success

(POSB: Introduction)

How does the world define success? How do you define it? What does it even mean to be successful? It does not matter whether you are rich or poor, educated or uneducated, saved or lost—everyone wants to be successful. There are many definitions of success. For some it means...

- making a lot of money
- getting a promotion at work
- making a lot of friends
- being needed by people
- becoming a community leader
- having degrees from the finest schools
- wearing the finest clothes
- driving the fanciest car
- owning the biggest house

And on and on. But the important question that demands our attention is this: How does God define success? God's definition of success does not depend on the external things of this world that impress men. When God thinks of success, He is thinking of faithfulness. True success is doing the will of God. Are you succeeding?

෴

PRACTICAL ILLUSTRATIONS

10-287

WITNESS

1 Timothy 4:6-16

(POSB: Note 7)

Confidence in the Truth

In witnessing, the fear of man is probably the most difficult factor for the Christian to overcome. Will he listen to me? Will he slam the door in my face? Will he laugh at me? Will he be offended? And so on. This timely story is taken from the pages of American history.

> Peter Cartwright, a nineteenth-century, circuit riding, Methodist preacher, was an uncompromising man. One Sunday morning when he was to preach, he was told that President Andrew Jackson was in the congregation, and was warned not to say anything out of line.
>
> When Cartwright stood to preach, he said, "I understand that Andrew Jackson is here. I have been requested to be guarded in my remarks. Andrew Jackson will go to hell if he doesn't repent."
>
> The congregation was shocked and wondered how the President would respond. After the service, President Jackson shook hands with Peter Cartwright and said, "Sir, if I had a regiment of men like you, I could whip the world."[75]

Are you more interested in guarding your remarks than you are in leading people to Christ?

10-288

WITNESS

1 Timothy 5:21-25

(POSB: Note 1)

A Delicate Operation

Are you the kind of person who pays close attention to details? As a believer in God's service you *should* be. You should respond in obedience to all the instructions that come from the Head of the Church, the Lord Jesus.

> When he was only a boy, French physician Alexis Carrel, Nobel Prize winner and one-time head of the Rockefeller Institute in New York, determined that he was going to be a surgeon. At a very early age he began to prepare his hands for the flexibility and suppleness necessary to perform delicate operations. One means was to secure the cover of a matchbox, place it over the two smallest fingers of either hand, and with a needle and suture...stitch the edges of cigarette paper together. Then he tied a fine knot in the suture to finish off the "operation"—all this in the narrow confines of that box top. As a surgeon he later amazed the medical world with his manipulative skill in the narrow recesses of the human body. Dr. Carrel's head was in complete mastery of his fingers.
>
> In the domain of the spiritual life we are frequently awkward because we have not allowed the Head, the Lord Jesus, to control our coordination and to teach us the

---

[75] Craig B. Larson, Editor. *Illustrations for Preaching & Teaching,* p.42.

possibilities of complete domination by our Lord....The world will never look at clumsy handlers of the problems of life, but will stop in some awe before the life that has trained itself...in the craft of Christian living. Men did not admire Carrel's fingers, they admired his head; men will not admire the man, but the Lord Jesus when they see your good works.[76]

You may be the only exposure some have to the gospel and the Christian life. Do others see Jesus in you? Do your actions point others to Christ?

ᕙᕗ

10-289

WITNESS

2 Timothy 3:10-13   **Godly Character**

(POSB: Introduction)

Would you consider yourself to be a godly believer? How can you really know for sure? An advertising poster for the United States Marines states: *"We're looking for a few good men!"* By that, the Marines put an emphasis on *quality* of character instead of *quantity* of people.

Much to the sorrow of Jesus Christ, many churches are filled with quantity instead of quality, with ungodly instead of godly people. In fact, at times it seems there is more of the world's influence in the church than the church's influence in the world.

As believers, we are under constant scrutiny by the world. Our character *is* our witness before others—whether godly or ungodly. How are you measuring up?

ᕙᕗ

10-290

WITNESS

2 Timothy 1:6-12   **A Life-Changing Gospel**

(POSB: Note 3)

Have you ever wondered why sharing the gospel seems to come so naturally to some people? The answer is simple: they live it every day, and everyone knows it. Listen to one striking example.

Radj (his friends called him Roger) was a college student who became a Christian in his home country of India. A zealous believer, Radj came to study in an American university. The English language was a constant challenge for Radj. Wanting to learn the language, Radj enlisted the help of a classmate named Billy. Billy was a young man comfortable with worldliness and unsure about spiritual things. Nevertheless, he was the closest friend Radj had in America. Thus Radj approached Billy and asked him to become his roommate and to teach him how to speak better English. Billy's answer caught Radj off-guard. "Roger, if I teach you English you'll make me a Christian."

---

[76] Donald Grey Barnhouse. *Let Me Illustrate*, p.66.

PRACTICAL ILLUSTRATIONS

"Explain," said Radj with a puzzled look in his eyes. "I just know that anyone who lives with you will become a Christian. They wouldn't stand a chance!"

Is the gospel that real in your life, real enough to change those who live with you, who work with you, who go to school with you?

❧

10-291

WITNESS

Titus 3:12-15

(POSB: Note 5)

Lost Opportunities

One of the key ingredients of successful evangelism is having a genuine burden for the lost. Listen to this story to see if your passion for souls exceeds that of this church member.

> One man came out of his house on the way to church on Sunday morning, just as his neighbor came out of his with his golf clubs. The golfer said, "Henry, come play golf with me today." Henry, with an expression of horror on his face replied, "This is the Lord's day, and I go to church. Certainly I would not play golf with you."
>
> After a moment's silence, the golfer quietly said, "You know Henry, I have often wondered about your church, and I have admired your fidelity. You know also that this is the seventh time I have invited you to play golf with me, and you have never invited me to go to church with you."[77]

Are you guilty of missing opportunities to witness? The world is lost. The Christian witness is desperately needed. If you don't do it, who will?

❧

10-292

WITNESS

1 Timothy 3:8-13

(POSB: Note 4, point 2)

The Power of the Holy Spirit

A person who is full of the Holy Spirit can be a powerful witness. But anyone who tries to do the Lord's work without the provision of God's Spirit will be sorely disappointed.

> Dr. Paul Brand was speaking to a medical college in India on "Let your light so shine before men that they may behold your good works and glorify your Father." In front of the lectern was an oil lamp, with its cotton wick burning from the shallow dish of oil. As he preached, the lamp ran out of oil, the wick burned dry, and the smoke made him cough. He immediately used the opportunity.

---

[77] Ted Kyle and John Todd, Compilers. *A Treasury of Bible Illustrations*, p. 395.

"Some of us here are like this wick," he said. "We're trying to shine for the glory of God, but we stink. That's what happens when we use ourselves as the fuel of our witness rather than the Holy Spirit.

"Wicks can last indefinitely, burning brightly and without irritating smoke, if the fuel, the Holy Spirit, is in constant supply."[78]

How much of God's work do you attempt to do without His power?

10-293

WITNESS

Titus 1:10-16

(POSB: Note 4)

A Ruined Testimony

The loudest sermons ever preached are those that are lived, not spoken. A false teacher will do everything in his power to speak like a Christian, but his works will betray him. For example:

Jerry worked in a clothing store during the week. To a casual acquaintance, Jerry would come across as a dedicated Christian. He was well versed in sounding "religious." But there was a strange contradiction in Jerry at work. If anyone wanted to know the latest gossip, Jerry was your man. If any backstabbing took place, Jerry was the source. If you wanted to find Jerry, the first place to look was in the break room. In other words, Jerry talked the talk but didn't walk the walk.

One day a fellow employee, Rick, had come to the end of his rope. Life had caved in on him and he was desperate for an answer. Sensing an opportunity to help, Jerry approached Rick and said, "Brother, what you need is religion." The broken man seethed in anger. Speaking in a voice that cracked with rage, he said "I'd rather die and go to hell than become a Christian if you are the best example they've got!"

Jerry's works had betrayed this broken man. Jerry's life denied the very reality that this man needed: the truth about Christ and the glorious salvation and life He gives to a person. Instead of accepting the Lord, Rick turned away—a choice based upon a ruined testimony—and looked for answers in all the wrong places.

Do your actions speak louder than your words? Do they confirm or deny your profession in Christ?

---

[78] Craig B. Larson, Editor. *Illustrations for Preaching & Teaching*, p.260.

PRACTICAL ILLUSTRATIONS

10-294

WOMEN

1 Timothy 2:9-15

(POSB: Note 4, point 3)

Living a Godly Life

Christian women should be examples of godliness not worldliness.

Corrie Ten Boom was a shining example of a godly woman. Even though she was captured and placed in a Nazi concentration camp during World War II, she would not compromise her testimony. In her book *The Hiding Place* she described what it was like to try to remain godly in such a terrible place. The guards would offer favors in exchange for sex. Some prisoners would give in out of desperation. For those who would not give in, conditions would worsen. It seemed unbearable, but Corrie held on to her faith in God.

Because she was determined to remain godly, the Lord was able to use her later to win many to Christ. She even became a celebrity and wrote her story, which later was made into a movie. Corrie spoke in many places around the world, telling of God's faithfulness in the most trying of times.

At one of these speaking engagements, a German man came up to meet her. He was visibly touched by her message of forgiveness. Corrie Ten Boom then had another chance to live what she preached. It was one of the most powerful and liberating moments of her godly life. The man explained that he remembered her from Germany, because he was one of the guards. He offered his hand and begged her forgiveness. Through the enabling of the Spirit, she reached out her hand and forgave the man.

What can God do through one woman determined to live a godly life? More than anyone could possibly imagine!

10-295

WORD OF GOD

2 Timothy 3:14-17

(POSB: Note 1)

The Benefit of Bible Study

Have you ever been lost for what seemed to be hours, when in fact your destination was only a block or a mile away? Think of the time wasted! How much time have you lost hunting for that "perfect verse" in the concordance of your Bible rather than just reading the Scriptures? Many times, we simply do not look hard enough in the right place, as happened to this couple:

A married couple checked into a nice hotel after driving all day. Exhausted and wishing to relax, they asked the clerk for the hotel's best room. Without hesitation, the clerk rang for the bellhop and handed over the key to room 710. Turning the key, the couple entered a room that was very nice but hardly worth the premium price they had paid. Not people to complain, they tipped the bellhop, pulled out the sofa-bed, and fell asleep, tossing and turning on the thin mattress.

PRACTICAL ILLUSTRATIONS

When the morning sun entered the room, the couple awoke with aching backs. Walking to the bathroom sink, the husband noticed a set of double doors. Curious, he said to his wife, "Honey, I just found the closet." Swinging the doors open, he was stunned! Inside the doors was the master bedroom suite. In the room were fresh-cut flowers and a basket of tasty fruit. Everything was beautiful: the furnishings, the curtains, the accessories down to the last detail. The man and wife stood there shaking their heads. "If only we had opened the door and entered in—all the way. We were only a few steps away from real comfort."

This married couple's frustration is typical of many Christian believers today. They fail to enter into God's Word all the way. They stop before they can get the full benefit of what He has to offer. Remember: you cannot really "live in" something until you are willing to go through the door!

10-296

WORD OF GOD

1 Timothy 4:6-16

(POSB: Note 2)

Do Not Settle for Substitutes

A wise minister, in fact, any believer, should know how to nourish his spirit by feeding on the food that will build him up. Nothing should ever be substituted for the Word of God, not if a person wishes to grow in Christ and minister to the needs of a lost and dying world.

The story is told of a cow that grew bored with the fenced-in grazing fields. He thought to himself, "I've fed off this pasture my whole life. I feel like a prisoner in this field...the grass sure does look greener on the other side."

As he probed the fence, he discovered a place where he could finally get through. With a hardy shove of his shoulder he was on the other side. Once there, he came eye-to-eye with another cow. "What brings you over here?" said the cow to his visitor. "I've come to try the grass on your side." "That's funny. I was just on my way to try the grass on your side. The grass over here is artificial. It looks real pretty until you try to take a bite!"

There are a lot of artificial substitutes available on the market today. Don't settle for anything less than the best, the Word of God.

PRACTICAL ILLUSTRATIONS

10-297

WORD OF GOD

1 Thessalonians 2:13-20

Fervor for God's Word

(POSB: Note 1)

How important is it to get God's Word into the hands of people? Think about it! So many of us are rich—we have several translations of Scripture on our bookshelves. Unfortunately, there are millions who do not have a copy of the precious Word of God. Listen to this stirring story of one man's attempt to reach the nations with God's Word. Let's call him Joe.

Joe was a member of an organization called The Gideons. The burden of the Gideons is to distribute God's Word so that people might read the Scriptures and make a decision to follow Christ. On one particular trip to a Far Eastern nation, a story began to unfold, a story that would be retold time and again.

On his trip, Joe had a suitcase of Testaments that he was eager to distribute. Never in his wildest dreams did he think he would run out before his trip was over. But there he was looking at a large group of young people. His heart sank as he quickly realized that there were more people than there were Bibles.

"God, what shall I do? There are not enough Testaments for all of these precious people." As Joe gazed into their faces, their eyes pierced his heart. He could sense their deep spiritual hunger for God—if only they could have God's Word.

"All right, Father. Which ones do you want to have a Bible?" Expecting God to indicate His choices with some visible sign, deep within his heart Joe heard this instead, "Joe, you select the ones. This is your responsibility, not Mine." And so, in obedience, Joe did the hardest thing he ever had to do in his life—decide who would and who would not receive God's Word.

Needless to say, this experience made a lasting impression on Joe's life. By the grace of God, never again would he be caught short of Testaments. Despite Joe's broken heart, God used him to distribute thousands of Testaments to people—people who went on to find Christ as Lord and Savior.

❧

10-298

WORD OF GOD

Titus 1:5-9

Getting Grounded in God's Word

(POSB: Note 4, point 2)

How confident are you in your ability to share the Word of God with other people? Suppose you won a ticket to be a contestant on a TV game show called "Bible Bonanza." Let's tune in and see how you might do. Okay, now. No help from the studio audience. You are on your own.

"Welcome to Bible Bonanza! Please welcome your host I.M. Smart."

"Thank you, thank you, thank you! Our finalist today is a member from your very own local church. Let's give a big welcome to Mrs. Bea Wright."

"Bea, you know the rules. Give me the right answer to this question and you win (drum roll please) 10 million dollars! All right, Bea, are you ready?"

PRACTICAL ILLUSTRATIONS

"Yes sir, Mr. Smart. I've been preparing for your show for years. I can't wait to start."
"Then let's begin. Bea, for 10 million dollars, give me book, chapter, and verse for six essential doctrines of the Christian faith."
"Uh, it sounds like a trick question to me. Wait, I know!
"Number 1: Dress nicely for church. From the book of First Fashions, chapter two, page 17.
"Number 2: Don't miss three Sunday School classes in a row. I'm sorry, I can't remember where I read that.
"Number 3: Be able to recite by heart John 3:15 'For God so loved'...or is it 1 John 3:16, 17...little John, John 3:18?"
HONK! "I'm sorry Bea, your time is up. You can forget that 10 million dollars but we have a consolation prize just for you. Your very own alarm clock. You need to wake up!"

Are you prepared to share God's Word or is it time for a wake-up call?

10-299

WORD OF GOD

2 Timothy 3:14-17   **God's Word: The Believer's Power**

(POSB: Note 5)

Can a new piano student play a symphony after only one lesson? Of course not. The student gets better by sitting on the piano bench day after day, playing the scales over and over again, and carefully learning every note on every bar of the sheet music. Studying the Scriptures is much the same. The more time you spend in God's Word, the more you get out of it, the more God blesses you and equips you to do His calling. Like the piano student who wants the symphony without the practice, too many Christians expect to get all the blessings promised in Scripture without spending time in God's Word. Based on the amount of time you spend in Scripture, are you more equipped to do God's work today than you were when you became a Christian?

10-300

WORD OF GOD

2 Timothy 2:8-13   **Hiding God's Word in Your Heart**

(POSB: Note 2)

Think for a moment. Can you think of any point in history when God's Word was snuffed out completely? You cannot, and that is the point. No one—no force, no evil, no government, not even Satan himself—can stop the gospel. The gospel finds a way, and it always will as seen in this example from World War II.

A few years...before the war, a humble villager in eastern Poland received a Bible from a colporteur [someone who sells or gives away Bibles] who visited a small hamlet. He read it, was converted, and passed the book on to others. Through that one Bible two hundred more [people] became believers.

PRACTICAL ILLUSTRATIONS

When the colporteur, Michael Billester, revisited the town in the summer of 1940, the group gathered to worship and listen to his preaching. Billester suggested that instead of giving the customary testimonies they all recite verses of Scripture.

Thereupon a man arose and asked, "Perhaps we have misunderstood. Did you mean verses or chapters?"

"Do you mean to say there are people here who can recite chapters of the Bible?" asked Mr. Billester in astonishment.

That was precisely the case. Those villagers had memorized, not only chapters, but also whole books of the Bible. Thirteen knew Matthew and Luke and half of Genesis. One had committed all the Psalms to memory. Together, the two hundred knew virtually the entire Bible. Passed around from family to family and brought to the gathering on Sundays, the old Book had become so worn with use that its pages were hardly legible.[79]

What is the best way to spread the Word of God? It is to internalize it, to hide it deep in your heart, and then to share it with those who need a word from God. Are you committed to do your part in keeping God's Word alive in your community?

☙

10-301
WORD OF GOD
1 Timothy 1:12-17   **An Irresistible Draw**
(POSB: Introduction)

We live in perilous times, days of gross immorality, lawlessness, and violence. Yet God has placed each believer in a strategic place, a place where the glorious power of the gospel must be proclaimed.

God's solution for the havoc produced by the false teachers of the world is to raise up true believers who are faithful to the gospel. Instead of responding to the tug of the false teacher's lies, the true believer is pulled by the irresistible draw of the Word of God—a pull that keeps him walking in the truth.

It was Edmund Burke who once commented, "The only thing necessary for the triumph of evil is for good men to do nothing."

Be determined to stand up for the truth. Tell of the marvelous truth of God's Word whenever, wherever, and to whomever He gives you the opportunity.

☙

10-302
WORD OF GOD
2 Timothy 3:14-17   **Living in God's Word**
(POSB: Introduction)

Educators tell us it takes about thirty consecutive days to make a habit stick. Through constant repetition, what at first seems awkward becomes second nature once a new habit is formed. Because we are fallen sinners,

---

[79] Paul Lee Tan. *Encyclopedia of 7,700 Illustrations: Signs of the Times*, p.196.

good habits are harder to form than bad habits. Bad habits just come naturally.

What good habits do you need to form? Chances are if you have a target, you will hit it. A very important target for the believer to hit is the Scriptures. It is in the Scriptures, the Word of God, where the habit of godliness is formed. But note: there are no short cuts to forming the habit of godliness. The Scriptures are not just a place where we drop in and visit from time to time. The Scriptures are to be lived in, to be dwelled in as if they were our very home. Are you willing to start out on a 30-day journey and form a good habit? There is no better time than the present to live in God's Word. The godly mark of a believer is that he lives in the Scriptures.

10-303

WORD OF GOD

2 Timothy 4:1-5

Sharing God's Word

(POSB: Introduction)

Who is supposed to preach the Word? A lot of believers delegate this job to their minister. After all, "Isn't that what we are paying him for?" But if the world is ever to be reached for Jesus Christ, it will take every Christian doing his part to share the good news. It was never God's intention to limit the preaching or sharing of God's Word to professional clergy. The job is too big and the message is too wonderful to delegate this task to just a few.

What keeps some believers from sharing the Word of God openly and freely? There are several reasons that cause people to hold back:

- the fear of being misunderstood
- the fear of being rejected
- the fear of not knowing all the answers
- shyness
- no passion for lost souls
- a lack of faithfulness
- a lack of obedience

The list could go on and on. But the point is this: if someone had not taken the time to share God's Word with you, where would you be right now? You would be lost, without hope.

The world is bombarded with messages offering hope for any and every area of life. But above all the messages and all the hopes that are laid out before us, there is one that is more needed by man than all the others—one that is so important that it supersedes all the others combined. What is that message? It is the message of the Word of God. The Word of God offers the only lasting hope for man. For this reason, the Word of God must be preached and taught. The believer must commit himself to the awesome charge of sharing the Word of God and ministering as never before.

10-304

WORK

1 Thessalonians 4:9-12

(POSB: Introduction)

The Believer's Job Description

Any organization worth its salt supplies a job description for its employees. A well-written job description allows the employee to know exactly what kind of work his employer is expecting from him. This crucial document of communication is a handy tool to have around when memories begin to fade from initial agreements.

In the same sense, God has given each believer a job description. Believers should:

- grow in love
- study to be quiet
- do their own business
- work with their own hands

This prescription, written down by the Apostle Paul centuries ago, works for every occupation.

❧

10-305

WORK

2 Thessalonians 3:6-18

(POSB: Introduction)

Diligence in the Workplace

Have you ever known someone so caught up in his or her work that family, health, and everything meaningful was neglected? How about the opposite extreme? Have you known or seen someone who was downright lazy, who had no ambition, no drive to achieve, produce, or provide? Unfortunately, society is full of both extremes. On one hand, you have workaholics. On the other hand, you have bums avoiding work. Both of these lifestyles or choices are wrong, but of the two, the latter is more strongly addressed by Scripture and is more prevalent in society.

The workplace is full of disorderly workers, workers who slack off and do as little as possible; workers who are men-pleasers, who work only when they see the boss coming. In addition to these, there are many in society who could be working, but who choose not to work due to selfishness, laziness, and lack of motivation. They have found ways to sponge off the government, social services, churches, and neighbors. The result is that a tragic dullness and a spirit of "give me, give me" have pervaded the workplace. But believers, above all others, should never be categorized as lazy. When it comes to diligence and hard work, we should be setting a dynamic example for others to follow.

❧

PRACTICAL ILLUSTRATIONS

10-306

WORK

1 Thessalonians 4:9-12

(POSB: Note 4)

Setting a Good Example

The Christian believer's work should speak for itself. A good test is this: When others look at the job you do, would they recommend you?

> Near the Kingsport Press in Tennessee a southbound bus [made] a scheduled mid-day stop of twenty minutes so that [the] passengers [could] freshen up and get a bite to eat.
>
> [The] driver said, as he brought the bus to a stop:
>
> "Folks, we'll be stopping here for twenty minutes. This line makes it a strict policy never to recommend an eating place by name, but if anybody wants me while we're here, I'll be eating a wonderful T-bone steak with French fries at Tony's first-class, spotlessly clean diner across the street.[80]

10-307

WORK

2 Thessalonians 3:6-18

(POSB: Note 2)

Staying Focused

The believer's work should remain focused and steady, a good example regardless of the habits of others.

> Ben and John worked as janitors for the same company. Ben felt his Christian testimony should be reflected in his work. John knew this as well, but never seemed to let that interfere with a good conversation.
>
> One day Ben was busily washing windows. John was busy too, busy talking to Ben. Ben wanted to stop and talk, but knew he had to stay focused to do a good job. He was soon glad he had resisted the temptation to goof off. In the reflection of the glass, he saw the supervisor walking up the stairs behind them. Ben continued to clean. John continued to talk. The boss continued to observe.
>
> Several minutes later, John turned and noticed the boss. He greeted him with a quick, "Oh, Hi," and moved along to his area. Later John asked "Ben, why didn't you tell me the boss was standing there?" "Well, not to sound mean or anything," Ben replied, "but Christ was standing there the whole time, and that didn't seem to bother you." John got the point and worked more faithfully from that point on.

How diligently are *you* working? Remember, the Lord *is* watching you!

---

[80] Donald Grey Barnhouse. Cited in: *Encyclopedia of 15,000 Illustrations.* Paul Lee Tan, Editor. (Dallas, TX: Bible Communications, Inc., 1998), #3297.

PRACTICAL ILLUSTRATIONS

10-308

Titus 2:1-10

(POSB: Note 7)

Whose Rules Do You Follow?

One of the greatest opportunities God gives His people is in the workplace. Our jobs provide the forum to present the claims of Christianity in a very graphic way—through our very lives.

> The pressure to conform to the "rules of the game" pressed on Randy's mind. Randy was a businessman who owned a paint and body shop. A lot of his business came from winning state and federal bids. If he did not win any bids, he would soon be out of business.
>
> On one particular day, Randy bid on a contract that would have provided plenty of cash to operate his business. Much to his disappointment, he lost the bid by several thousand dollars to a company in another state. As he re-studied his bid, something just did not add up. He felt that the company that won the bid must have used the wrong specifications or done some misfiguring, and if so, they were going to take a huge loss. Randy took the risk of being misunderstood and called the sales representative who won the bid. "I've looked at my figures and the job specifications. Are you sure your bid is right?" The sales representative had met Randy at a trade show a few years earlier and had been impressed by his character. While other men were cutting corners with the truth, Randy had always been very up-front with him. As he checked back over his figures, his heart sank into his stomach. "Randy, thank you for watching out for me. This would have ruined my business. There is still time for me to call and cancel my bid."

Randy could have done several things. He could have…

- ignored the terrible mistake of his competitor
- taken advantage of the situation for his own gain
- ridiculed his competitor

But Randy did the right thing. Being a competitor did not excuse him from doing what was right—even in the workplace. What set of rules do you follow in the workplace?

❧

10-309

1 Timothy 6:1-2

(POSB: Note 1)

Work as Unto the Lord

The believing employee has a unique opportunity to turn his or her employer to Christ by what he does—and doesn't do—on the job and how he does it.

> Russ was a crusty man who prided himself on pushing people until they quit or struck out against him. As store manager, he had a pretty good bark and held the power to bite when it served his purpose.
>
> Harold was a mild-mannered fellow who got along with everybody. When he started his job, every employee warned him about Russ. Nevertheless, Harold decided to let

the quality of his work speak for itself. Harold loved Jesus a lot. And he knew the thing that would please Christ the most would be to give his best effort to Russ.

At first, Russ ignored Harold's work. But that did not bother Harold. For in reality, Harold was not working for Russ but for the Lord. Over the course of time, Harold proved to be a very valuable employee. The quality of his work did not taper off. In fact, with added experience, his work actually improved.

Being a man whose chief interest was results, Russ began to take a serious interest in Harold. One day Russ said to Harold, "Harold, what is it that makes you tick?" Seeing an open door Harold responded, "Russ, I'm a Christian." Russ just scoffed. "I've hired and fired a bunch of Christians and they have not impressed me one little bit. What makes you so different?"

Harold thought about his question for a few moments. He squinted his eyes as if that would squeeze out a good answer. "Russ, I guess the difference is that I not only love the Lord and want to please Him, but I also want to love and please you. I figure that if I please Him, He will take care of pleasing you."

Do you work to please the Lord? The quality of your work should say so—loud and clear. It should be good enough that others will take notice.

10-310

WORK
1 Timothy 6:3-5   **Wrong Motives in the Ministry**
(POSB: Note 5, point 2)

A person does not choose the ministry; God chooses the minister. A person should only enter the ministry if he has been truly called by the Lord.

A middle-aged farmer who had been desiring for years to be an evangelist was out working in the field one day when he decided to rest under a tree. As he looked into the sky he saw that the clouds seemed to form into the letters P and C. Immediately he hopped up, sold his farm, and went out to P-reach C-hrist, which he felt was God's leading. Unfortunately, he was a horrible preacher. After one of his sermons, a neighbor came forward and whispered in his ear, "Are you sure God wasn't just trying to tell you to P-lant C-orn?"[81]

81 Michael P. Green. *1500 Illustrations for Biblical Preaching.* (Grand Rapids, MI: Baker Books, 2000), #1460.

TOPICAL
INDEX

SUBJECT	SCRIPTURE	PAGE

SUBJECT	SCRIPTURE	PAGE

SUBJECT	SCRIPTURE	PAGE

OUTLINE BIBLE RESOURCES

This material, like similar works, has come from imperfect man and is thus susceptible to human error. We are nevertheless grateful to God for both calling us and empowering us through His Holy Spirit to undertake this task. Because of His goodness and grace, *The Preacher's Outline & Sermon Bible*® New Testament is complete, and Old Testament volumes are releasing periodically.

The Minister's Personal Handbook and other helpful **Outline Bible Resources** are available in printed form as well as releasing electronically on WORDsearch software.

God has given the strength and stamina to bring us this far. Our confidence is that as we keep our eyes on Him and grounded in the undeniable truths of the Word, we will continue working through the Old Testament volumes. The future includes other helpful Outline Bible Resources for God's dear servants to use in their Bible Study and discipleship.

We offer this material first to Him in whose Name we labor and serve and for whose glory it has been produced and, second, to everyone everywhere who preaches and teaches the Word.

Our daily prayer is that each volume will lead thousands, millions, yes even billions, into a better understanding of the Holy Scriptures and a fuller knowledge of Jesus Christ the Incarnate Word, of whom the Scriptures so faithfully testify.

You will be pleased to know that Leadership Ministries Worldwide partners with Christian organizations, printers, and mission groups around the world to make Outline Bible Resources available and affordable in many countries and foreign languages. It is our goal that *every* leader around the world, both clergy and lay, will be able to understand God's Holy Word and present God's message with more clarity, authority, and understanding—all beyond his or her own power.

LEADERSHIP MINISTRIES WORLDWIDE
PO Box 21310 • Chattanooga, TN 37424-0310
423) 855-2181 • FAX (423) 855-8616
info@outlinebible.org
www.outlinebible.org - FREE Download materials

LEADERSHIP MINISTRIES WORLDWIDE

Publishers of Outline Bible Resources

Currently Available Materials, with New Volumes Releasing Regularly

- **THE PREACHER'S OUTLINE & SERMON BIBLE® (POSB)**

NEW TESTAMENT

Matthew I (chapters 1-15)	1 & 2 Corinthians
Matthew II (chapters 16-28)	Galatians, Ephesians, Philippians, Colossians
Mark	1 & 2 Thess., 1 & 2 Timothy, Titus, Philemon
Luke	Hebrews, James
John	1 & 2 Peter, 1, 2, & 3 John, Jude
Acts	Revelation
Romans	Master Outline & Subject Index

OLD TESTAMENT

Genesis I (chapters 1-11)	1 Kings	Jeremiah 1 (chapters 1-29)
Genesis II (chapters 12-50)	2 Kings	Jeremiah 2 (chapters 30-52),
Exodus I (chapters 1-18)	1 Chronicles	Lamentations
Exodus II (chapters 19-40)	2 Chronicles	Ezekiel
Leviticus	Ezra, Nehemiah, Esther	Daniel/Hosea
Numbers	Job	Joel, Amos, Obadiah, Jonah,
Deuteronomy	Proverbs	Micah, Nahum
Joshua	Ecclesiastes, Song of Solomon	Habakkuk, Zephaniah, Haggai,
Judges, Ruth	Isaiah 1 (chapters 1-35)	Zechariah, Malachi
1 Samuel	Isaiah 2 (chapters 36-66)	*New volumes release periodically*
2 Samuel		

KJV Available in Deluxe 3-Ring Binders or Softbound Edition • NIV Available in Softbound Only

- **The Preacher's Outline & Sermon Bible New Testament — 3 Vol. Hardcover • KJV – NIV**

- *What the Bible Says to the Believer* — **The Believer's Personal Handbook**
  11 Chs. – Over 500 Subjects, 300 Promises, & 400 Verses Expounded - Italian Imitation Leather or Paperback

- *What the Bible Says to the Minister* — **The Minister's Personal Handbook**
  12 Chs. - 127 Subjects - 400 Verses Expounded - Italian Imitation Leather or Paperback

- **Practical Word Studies In the New Testament** — 2 Vol. Hardcover Set

- **The Teacher's Outline & Study Bible™ - Various New Testament Books**
  Complete 30 - 45 minute lessons – with illustrations and discussion questions

- **Practical Illustrations** — **Companion to the POSB**
  Arranged by topic and Scripture reference

- **What the Bible Says Series – Various Subjects**
  Prayer • The Passion • The Ten Commandments • The Tabernacle

- **Software – Various products powered by WORDsearch**
  New Testament • Pentateuch • History • Prophets • Practical Word Studies • Various Poetry/Wisdom

- **Topical Sermons Series – Available online only**
  7 sermons per series • Sermons are from the Preacher's Outline & Sermon Bible

- **Non-English Translations of various books**
  Included languages are: Russian – Spanish – Korean – Hindi – Chinese – Bulgarian – Romanian –
  Malayalam – Nepali – Italian – Arabic
  • Future: French, Portuguese

— Contact LMW for Specific Language Availability and Prices —

For quantity orders and information, please contact:
LEADERSHIP MINISTRIES WORLDWIDE or Your Local Christian Bookstore
PO Box 21310 • Chattanooga, TN 37424-0310
(423) 855-2181 (9am – 5pm Eastern) • FAX (423) 855-8616
E-mail - info@outlinebible.org Order online at www.outlinebible.org

PURPOSE STATEMENT

LEADERSHIP MINISTRIES WORLDWIDE

exists to equip ministers, teachers, and laymen in their understanding, preaching and teaching of God's Word by publishing and distributing worldwide *The Preacher's Outline & Sermon Bible*® and related **Outline Bible Resources**, to reach & disciple men, women, boys and girls for Jesus Christ.

MISSION STATEMENT

1. To make the Bible so understandable – its truth so clear and plain – that men and women everywhere, whether teacher or student, preacher or hearer, can grasp its message and receive Jesus Christ as Savior, and...

2. To place the Bible in the hands of all who will preach and teach God's Holy Word, verse by verse, precept by precept, regardless of the individual's ability to purchase it.

Outline Bible Resources have been given to LMW for printing and especially distribution worldwide at/below cost, by those who remain anonymous. One fact, however, is as true today as it was in the time of Christ:

THE GOSPEL IS FREE, BUT THE COST OF TAKING IT IS NOT

LMW depends on the generous gifts of believers with a heart for Him and a love for the lost. They help pay for the printing, translating, and distributing of **Outline Bible Resources** into the hands of God's servants worldwide, who will present the Gospel message with clarity, authority, and understanding beyond their own.

LMW was incorporated in the state of Tennessee in July 1992 and received IRS 501 (c)(3) nonprofit status in March 1994. LMW is an international, nondenominational mission organization. All proceeds from USA sales, along with donations from donor partners, go directly to underwrite our translation and distribution projects of **Outline Bible Resources** to preachers, church and lay leaders, and Bible students around the world.